The Life and Times of
Berwick-upon-Tweed

'A town neither wholly regulated by English or Scottish laws, but by customs and usages in some things differing from both, yet rather inclined to English laws, and more affecting Scottish fashions and language, as being oftener saluted by the rescript of the one, and seeing and hearing of the other.'

The Recorder of Berwick, to King Charles I
at his visit to the town, 6 June 1633.

The Life and Times of
Berwick-upon-Tweed

RAYMOND LAMONT-BROWN

JOHN DONALD PUBLISHERS LTD
EDINBURGH

ISBN 0 85976 233 5

Phototypesetting by Print Origination Ltd., Formby.
Printed by Bell & Bain Ltd., Glasgow.

Acknowledgements

This book is the culmination of many years of research and is the result of personal investigation, both as a resident of Berwick and as an exile. The author would particularly like to record gratitude for the useful conversations with the late Rev. H. Stanley Ross of Spittal and the late Rev. Dr. L.O. Henderson of Tweedmouth who both guided on-the-spot research. Also many conversations with the members of the Berwick Local History Society and the Berwickshire Naturalists' Club are put on record, as is a thanks to Mr F.M. Cowe of Berwick for past comments. Individually the following have been of particular assistance: Christina Hunter Robertson, Librarian and Archivist, the Royal Bank of Scotland; B.R. Taylor, Branch Manager, TSB Bank, Berwick; G.F. Miles, Archivist, Barclays Bank PLC; D.B. Inns, Public Information Office, House of Commons; Alan Cameron, Archivist, Bank of Scotland; Robin Gard, Hon. Editor, North East Catholic Historical Society, Newcastle; John Slater, Editor, *Railway Magazine*; Ronnie Tait, General Manager, Lindisfarne Ltd; Ian Copland, District Librarian, NE Fife District Council; R.D. Steward, Deputy County Archivist, Northumberland County Council; the staff of Berwick Museum; the staff of Berwick Public Library; the staff of the University Library, University of St Andrews; Miss J. West of the Ordnance Survey; R. Swell, School of Oriental and African Studies, University of London; Michael M. Chrimes, Librarian, Institution of Civil Engineers; and my good friend of many years, W.A. Montgomery of Berwick.

The author's thanks also go to John R. Reay, Secretary of the Guild of Freemen for assistance in tracing the Guild's history, and to the Freemen for permission to quote from their *Notes* (1968).

St Andrews, 1988.   *Raymond Lamont-Brown.*

Contents

CHAPTER 1

Out of the Celtic Twilight

The River Tweed and its tributaries penetrate deeply into the hill country between the Cheviots and the Lammermuirs sculpted during the Ice Ages. Around 10,000 years ago, the glaciers of the last Ice Age melted and plants began to colonise the land, followed by grazing animals and meat-devouring predators, of which one type was early man. Into this land around 9000 BC people started to migrate from the South and from across the North Sea to till the land with their digging sticks and hoes which had first been invented in western Asia. Berwick's hinterland has, over the last century of archaeological research, produced evidence of the earliest settlements of the Middle Stone Age (c.3000 BC) and the hunter-fishers of the New Stone Age (c.2500 BC) with their axes and polished hammers of stone. In those days there was much more woodland around Berwick and the weather was warmer and drier than it is now.

In the late Bronze Age, some 3500 years ago, the descendants of those early peoples were joined in the moorlands and valleys about modern Berwick by the migrants who came from as far away as Yorkshire with their distinctive pots and beakers. They hunted the woods, they scoured the scrubland and savoured the riches of the burns, water-meadows and fertile plateaux of the Tweed Valley. It was a land of roe deer and wild boar, beavers, wolves, bears and wild cattle. Great auks, cranes, grouse, blackcock and capercailzie were plentiful, as were sheep, goats and horses which had come to live here long before 4000 BC, brought maybe in dugout boats from the Continent. From some kind of centre at Rothbury these folk left their curious cup and ring carvings to mark their passage.

By the mid-first century BC, the Iron Age folk from the south mingled here as colonists and stabilised the economy from their multivallate defences. Their centres were at such places as

1

Cockburn Law and Earn's Heugh, Habchester at the west end
of Lamberton Moor, Edin's Hall and Dirrington Great Law.
Many of these sites were founded on much older hill forts which
had appeared by 800 BC. Up to the coming of the Romans these
peoples settled largely in individual steadings cultivating common land and only used the forts as places of refuge rather than
continually inhabited sites. But it must be remembered that the
Bronze Age lasted late in Northumberland, for when the
Romans came the inhabitants around the Tweed's mouth and
middle reaches were still exponents of the Bronze Age culture.
They lived mostly in their thatch and wattle huts and were
mobile on the Tweed in their logboats.

All this we can glean from the *Geography of Ptolemy*, the great
work of Claudius Ptolemaeus of Alexandria, the astronomer
and founder of scientific cartography. Ptolemy lived during the
days of Hadrian and Marcus Aurelius, that is round about 140
AD, and from his writings and other classical sources it can be
seen that what is now Berwick—by the time Britain became a
province of Rome following the conquest of 43 AD—was
within the territory of the tribe known as the Votadini. Traprain
Law in East Lothian was the great *oppidum* (native town) of the
Votadini and the site was occupied until the fifth century. Ptolemy also mentions High Rochester in Upper Redesdale—
which the Romans called *Bremenium*—as a 'main city' of the
Votadini. The tribe also worked out of the hill forts first established in the Iron Age.

The bilingual Votadini spoke Gaelic and Brittonic, the latter a
language related to modern Welsh. Their activities in the hills
about Berwick's modern site concerned the tilling of the land
and the tending of sheep for wool for such clothes as those
woollen cloaks mentioned in Diocletian's edict *De Maximus
Pretiis*. Without a doubt they fished the Tweed and knew the
coastal region well.

The Roman military advance into what they called the *civitas
Votadinorum* was conducted by 80 AD by the governor of
Britannia, Gnaeus Julius Agricola. As a consequence a great
main Roman route into Scotland called Dere Street was estab-

lished from *Eburacum* (York) to cut through the Votadini territory, leaving the Tweed at *Trimontium* (Newstead) to drive
through to the Forth. Just north of the Roman headquarters of
the *ala Petriana* (a 1000-strong cavalry regiment) at *Corstopitum*
(Corbridge), at Bewclay, another Roman road branched to the
east. Traditionally it is called the Devil's Causeway and it makes
its way to Berwick. This Roman road peters out just south of
Scremerston Hill, but it lines up with the site of the old ford
across the Tweed (west of Berwick's new road bridge bypass). In
his *Caledonia* (1807), George Chalmers says that the road
crossed the Tweed near West Ord and went towards
Mordington. He quotes William Roy's *The Military Antiquities of
the Romans in Britain* (1793), saying: 'This road may possibly have
communicated with the Roman station on the Whiteadder,
near Allanbank....'; furthermore he says that Ainslie's map
carried the road forward to St Abb's Head. The Devil's
Causeway also linked a 'short cut' from *Bremenium* to Berwick,
via *Alauna* (Learchild) to the west of modern Alnwick.

Today there is no sign of a Roman fort at Berwick, and
perhaps there was nothing more here in Roman times than a
signal station. It is almost certain that the area we now call
Berwick would be a base for the Roman *exploratores*—the
frontier surveyor-rangers—or the *arcani*—the frontier scouts;
their presence might be attested archaeologically, inferred
from the pottery found at Sunnyside, south of Tweedmouth.
Work has been done in recent years at Doubstead, near
Scremerston, on a Romano-British site, and the Roman British
settlements at Chester Hill and Greenfield Plantation would
suggest a back-up service of trade and supplies for the
exploratores. The fact that the Roman road came to the mouth of
the Tweed would suggest too that the area was deemed of some
importance and maybe under Berwick's quay lie the wooden
supports of a Roman jetty from which the imperial fleet were
serviced on their way to *Bodotria Aest* (the Firth of Forth). A rare
memory of this may be referred to in a fragment of a verse
collected in 1834 by Alexander Carr, author of the *History of
Coldingham Priory*:

Sin' the days o' Gilligacus
There's been fishers on the Tweed:
Sin' the Romans came to wrack us,
And consume our ancient seed;
A castle strong, has been to back us
On the tap o' yon brae head.

(*Galgacus*: Caledonian chief, c. 85 AD).

It is likely that the Votadini chieftains had special privileges under the Roman occupation and only harried the Romans in an opportunistic way. But by the 360s AD the *Picti* were ravaging the territory north of Hadrian's Wall. The Picts were the descendants of the people who had built the hillforts, and most of our information about them comes from the Romans: they were introduced to us for the first time by the Latin panegyrist, Eumenius, c.297.

The coastlands in particular saw the activities of attacks from the Scots, the Attacotti and the Saxons. The abandoning of Hadrian's Wall, some time after 385 AD, led to the end of the Roman military occupation of Britain around 406 AD, and the beginning of the post-Roman kingdoms. The role of kingship evolved slowly, and any settlement at Berwick would have had as its main purpose the feeding of the local 'king' and his warriors.

The lands of the Votadini to the north of modern Berwick were known in Early Christian times as the frontier of Gododdin, and by the sixth century the region was dominated by the rise of Bernicia and the Anglian advance. Berwick is likely to have been part of an area of suzerainty of a local 'king' whose lands lay from about the Lammermuirs to Alnwick, with Bamburgh and the Millfield Basin as main settlement areas. All the time, it must be remembered, raiders came and went as they pleased in search of cattle and slaves; from 360 AD to 450 AD the Scots and Picts raided northern England for their human booty. By 500 AD Germanic mercenaries and settlers began to appear around the mouth of the Tweed.

In his *Historia Britonum*, Nennius the chronicler tells us that the kingdom of Bernicia was founded by King Ida 'The Flamebearer' in 547 AD. This Anglo-Saxon kingdom stretched

from the Tyne to the Forth, and in 604 AD Aethelfrith united
the Saxon independent kingdom of Deira with Bernicia to form
one kingdom. Indeed it was at the battle of Degsastan (modern
Addinston, Berwickshire) in 603 AD between Aedan
MacGabran, King of Scots and Aethelfrith, that the latter
established Anglian supremacy over this area. Two flourishing
settlements now dominated the area, one at Bamburgh and the
other at Yeavering. On Aethelfrith's death in 616 AD his
kingdom was absorbed by Edwin his brother-in-law, and he
seized the throne of Northumbria in 617 AD. In 634 AD
Oswald, King of the Northumbrians, conquered Bernicia and
gave Lindisfarne to Aidan, the missionary bishop from Iona;
Lindisfarne was to be the see of Aidan's bishopric. By 638 AD
the whole of the lands that had been the Votadini territory north
of the Tweed were absorbed into Northumbria by war and
conquest by the successors of Edwin. In time the
Northumbrian kings were forced to acknowledge the
independence of the Scottish kings of Dalriada and the British
kings of Strathclyde. Northumbrian fortunes waxed and waned
as Christianity became prevalent in the lands of North
Northumbria and the Southeast Borders, large parts of which
were settled on the church. Ealdormen—nobles of the highest
rank—now ruled the northern marches on behalf of the king.
The territorial domain of Northumbria known as
Norhamshire and Islandshire was established around 635 AD.

Christianity, by the by, first came to Pictland around 565 AD
when Columba and other missionaries from Ireland settled at
Iona. The Picts, who were followers of Columba's Celtic
Church, were often at war with their southern neighbours the
Northumbrians, who had adopted the practices of the Roman
Church. There were differences between Celtic and Roman
churches on issues such as the calculation of the date of Easter,
the tonsure and so on. When part of southern Pictland was lost
to the Northumbrians in 658 AD it came under the influence of
the Roman Church. In 710 AD King Nechtan was converted to
Roman practices which were to become firmly rooted in
Pictland. The influence and power of the church was reflected

in the interesting mobility of Northumbrians, and the mobility of the later medieval merchants and craftsmen from Berwick was begun around this period, for we see Northumbrian glaziers working on St Peter's Church, Restenneth Priory, Angus, at this time.

By the sixth century the centre of activity was south of modern Berwick which was only peripheral to events, for if it had any relevance at all it was no more than that of a monastic grange, a *villa frumentaria*(see page 191). Buildings at the *villa* would be timber-framed with wattle walls and thatched roofs. Beef cattle, sheep, pigs and horses would all be bred, with the hunting of boar, salmon-fishing and seal-hunting to augment the diet; skin-covered boats too would scud across the Tweed. Barley also may have been farmed as a part of the staple diet, as Bede mentions its cultivation at Lindisfarne in his *Life*.

It may be noted at this point that there are references to a Saxon village called Bondington on the outskirts of the medieval site of Berwick. Probably it was in the region of Castle Terrace and had a church(see page 38), and cottages and acres which belonged to the monks of Kelso for the *Kelso Chartulary* tells us so. It is likely that this village was the focal point of dwellings before 1000 AD and that the Berwick we know today was no more than a fishing haven. In time, of course, Bondington was to vanish as Berwick flourished.

Certainly any early settlement at Berwick was of no consequence to Bede who was gathering material for his *History* around 693-731 AD; if it had been he would surely have mentioned it when describing his *Urbs Coluda* (an early monastic site which was probably Coldingham).

Lindisfarne was the scene of the first Danish attack on the East Coast. The monastery was sacked in 793 AD and most of the monks were murdered. The monastery survived until the next Danish onslaught of 875 AD, when the monks and their bishop, Eardulph, left the island for ever. Whatever settlements were at Berwick between 793 AD and 875 AD would have received the attention of the Danes and been pillaged; probably the mouth of the Tweed was used as a shelter by the Danes.

From 876 AD to 954 AD the Kingdom of Northumbria was largely controlled by the Danes and the area was subject to increasing activity by Scandinavian settlers, the centre of whose world was at *Yorvic* (York). Such writers as J.Scott quote Peter de Longtoff's *Metrical Chronicle* of the fourteenth century as saying that Oseth, King of the Danes, arrived at Berwick in 833 AD. If this is the case, the entry could be the earliest notice of Berwick anywhere, but its credence is disputable.

Writing in 1833 John Sykes, who prepared the volume *Local Records*, quotes Hector Boece's unsubstantiated entry for the year 872 AD: 'Gregory, King of Scotland, who was contemporary with Alfred, took Berwick by assault. The garrison consisted of Danes and Picts; the former he put to the sword, but spared the latter. The King of Scots pursued the Danes into Northumberland, where he defeated them, then returned to Berwick and passed the winter'.

The Anglo-Saxon law and land divisions rule, under which the Berwick settlement would come, developed from Danelaw (the law which prevailed from the ninth to the eleventh centuries in the land north of Watling Street) to Wapentakes (similar to the southern 'hundreds' of 100 familes), to Carucates (as much land as a team of oxen could plough in a season) to the Duodecimal System (in which land was divided into twelfth parts).

Whichever chronicler is to be believed, it can be said for sure that the Bernicians who lived in the Berwick region would find themselves caught between two powerful and expanding peoples: the Scottish dynasty north of the Forth and the Danes to the south. The Bernicians changed sides regularly in order to survive. So by the ninth century the Scots were annexing Lothian and pushing ambitiously towards the Tweed.

In 840 AD Edgar surrendered East Lothian to Kenneth and Saxon Berwick went to Scotland. The St Albans monk, Robert de Wendover, Prior of Belvoir, who died in 1236, writes in his *Flores Historiarum* that the Danes, Inguar and Ubba, wreaked vengeance at Berwick. In 950 AD the Saxon, Edred, grandson of Alfred the Great, subdued Northumberland and abolished the old kingdom and appointed the first Earl of Northumberland with a centre at the old 'city' and royal capital at Bamburgh. By around 973 AD the Durham tract *De Primo Saxonum Adventu* (c.1100) tells us that Edgar of Wessex received the homage of Kenneth II of Scotland who was granted Lothian in return. By and large the years 950 AD to 1050 AD were a century of tranquillity, despite the second Danish invasion which made Cnut the Dane (1017-35) king by conquest and election.

In Scotland at the turn of the tenth century, Malcolm II Mackenneth (1005-34) had established his rule as King of the Picts and Scots and he continued the aggression in the south which had been begun by his predecessors. For in the ninth century the nascent kingdom of the Scots had laid claim to all the land between Forth and Tweed: throughout the tenth century the Scots tried to dominate the *heah-gerefa* (high reeves), then the Earls of Bamburgh. Although he was repulsed at Durham in 1006, Malcolm defied the Northumbrian army of Earl Uhtred at Carham in 1018 and secured Scottish control over East Lothian as far as the Tweed—the inference is that it was Scottish territory anyway—which he now formally claimed as Scottish along with Berwick. At Carham Malcolm was assisted, says the *Historia Regum*, by 'Owen the Bald, king of the men of the Clyde' (*Eugenius Calvus rex Clutinensium*). In his *Historia Dunelmensis Ecclesiae* Symeon of Durham says 'the entire people, from the river Tees to the Tweed, with their nobility almost wholly perished'. There is no record that Berwick was pillaged at this time; but as Malcolm claimed it, it is unlikely that he would sack it; a further clue that Berwick was already 'in the hands of the Scots' is that no recorded sacking infers no organised opposition. Around the year 1030, Skene records in *Celtic Scotland*, a war fleet was fitted out at Berwick by Duncan, grandson of Malcolm II.

Although Malcolm had to submit to Cnut in 1031, it appears that the Scots still held Berwick by Cnut's favour. By this time the Tweed was confirmed as a 'natural frontier' between England and Scotland, but the Border remained very undetermined.

The focus of Bamburgh as a power base in the north did decline and a rather dilapidated Saxon 'city' remained until the coming of the Normans in 1066. By 1045 Berwick was in the earldom of Siward, and after 1065 was the responsibility of Oswulf. But it was Bamburgh rather than Berwick that historians identify as 'the corner of Northumberland defended on all sides by the sea and marshes' which William I, the Conqueror (1066-87), set out to subdue in his attempt to conquer the North. The Normans are recorded in Scotland from 1052. In reality there was no Norman conquest of Scotland. Normanisation of Scotland came through marriage rather than by feat of arms; for instance William I's son married Malcolm Canmore's daughter. In David I's reign the Normans came to Scotland as advisors, clerics, administrators and as guests. Bamburgh was to be the effective limit of the Norman conquest of the North. But William did lead forays across the Tweed, returning with 'great booty'.

One important effect of William's policy was to make refugees of Edgar the Aetheling, grandson of Edmund Ironside, and his two sisters. They fled to the court of Malcolm III (1058-93), surnamed Canmore or 'Big Head', who had come to the throne of Scotland after his victory over Macbeth in 1057. Edgar's sister, Margaret, married the widowed Malcolm III and the marriage had two important consequences. First, it led, through Margaret's influence, to the anglicisation of the Lothians, and secondly, it gave Malcolm the pretext to raid England, ostensibly to redress the wrongs done to his brother-in-law. So Malcolm undertook no fewer than five invasions of England between 1061 and 1093. But, by 1072 the Normans broke through Scottish resistance and Ailred of Rievaulx noted that Malcolm was forced to pay homage to William I at Abernethy. (In his *Chronica Majora*, the Benedictine chronicler Matthew Paris says the homage was at Berwick, but this is unlikely.) Bypassing the possibility of fortifying Berwick—still a Scottish town—the Normans built a *ville neuve* ('New Castle') on the Tyne, and William Rufus, now king after his father's death in 1087, invaded Scotland to stop the incursions of 1091. The

long and short of it was that Malcolm was defeated and became
William Rufus's 'leige man' and Rufus continued his
subjugation of the south-west Borders.

All that can be said for sure is that by the eleventh century
Berwick was *in existence*. There is no reliable reference
whatsoever before the ninth century to tell us if Berwick was
Saxon or Norse, for the Saxon *Berwici* and the Norse *Barevik* are
of equal credence. Was Bondington where the Saxons lived and
Barevik where the Norse invaders lived separately? We shall
never know. But Berwick begins to be mentioned in chronicles
that may be considered reliable. John of Fordun, the chantry
priest and Canon of Aberdeen, tells us that in 1097, Edgar, King
of Scotland, gave lands in 'the village of Berwick' to the
monastery of Coldingham. As a cross-reference we can note
that Ralph Holinshed in his *Chronicles of England Scotlande and
Irelande* (1577) puts it a little differently; he says that Edgar gave
'the village of Berwick with all its appurtenances' to Carileph,
Bishop of Durham, in honour of St Cuthbert who had
appeared to him in a dream before he vanquished Donald
Bane. Holinshed says that Edgar carried the banner of St
Cuthbert into battle. Carileph's successor, Ranulph
Flambard—builder of Norham Castle in 1121—Holinshed
continues, spurned Edgar's gift of Berwick and, during Edgar's
absence from Scotland at the English court, invaded Scotland
to return to Durham 'laden with the spoil of the plundered Borders'. Edgar appealed to William Rufus for restitution and
claimed back the town of Berwick. By the end of the eleventh
century, it may be noted, Berwick was being used as the name
for the shire capital north of the Tweed.

At the start of the twelfth century Berwick would be English in
speech and broadly Anglo-Scandinavian in culture, with a dash
of Votadinian blood in the Anglian strain. Edgar was succeeded
in 1107 by Alexander I who strengthened his ties with England,
marrying Sibylla, a natural daughter of Henry I of England.
Alexander in turn was succeeded in 1124 by David I who, like
his brothers Edgar and Alexander, had received an English
education at Henry's court. Henry's reign had given political

stability to England, but David was to cause disruption in the North and bring Berwick significantly into history.

Berwick's development would be a slow process, and the factors that led to prominence would be threefold. First, there was its geographical position as the boundary between England and Scotland. Then there was its good harbourage served by important approach roads to a bridged crossing. And, finally, it was a convenient point for exchange and marketing. The taking of the town by the Scots was always an economic necessity because it served a huge hinterland. When the English took the town it was a preventive move to deny its use by the Scots.

David of Scotland was a feudal monarch in the Anglo-Norman tradition and was more Norman than his predecessors. His marriage to Matilda of Huntingdon brought him English titles and English wealth, and he embarked on a policy of Norman-type administration both at burgh and ecclesiastical levels. David founded a wide range of religious communities in Scotland from Selkirk in 1113 to Jedburgh in 1118. He endowed the Benedictine monks from Tiron in their abbey at Selkirk (removed to Kelso around 1128) with possessions in Berwick, as is recorded in the *Selkirk Abbey Charter* (1113-9), including a house, fishing rights, and the use of a mill.

Cistercian wool came down the Tweed for shipment at Berwick, and with this trade came prosperity. Already large properties and important rights in Berwick were in ecclesiastical hands; for instance, the Augustinians of Holyrood owned fishing rights at Berwick, the Tironesians of Lindores had tofts in the town, and the monks of Dunfermline and Jedburgh owned *mansurae* within the burgh. In 1261 Abbot Matthew of Melrose is quoted as supervising the building of 'our great houses at Berwick'.

Around the year 1120 David made Berwick a royal burgh within the Court of Four Burghs (*Curia Quattuor Burgorum*: the other royal burghs were Roxburgh, Edinburgh and Selkirk). The court decided questions involving the usages of burghs, the rights and duties of the burgesses, how taxes were levied and so on. From this point the town's reputation began to spread.

There is evidence of this a hundred miles to the north. In St Andrews, Bishop Robert founded the Augustinian Priory in 1144 and thereafter set about establishing a burgh with the permission of the king on the already settled headland around the religious community of Kinrimund. This he had done by the 1150s. Bishop Robert sought for its civic head in Berwick, and chose as the first provost (*praepositus*) of St Andrews an opulent wool merchant (*proprius burgensis*) called Maynard the Fleming. The employment of burghers, craftsmen and clerks from Berwick continued, and by the thirteenth century many had risen to very high office. For instance the *Calendar of the Close Rolls, 1288-96* records how John of Berwick, a clerk, was an executor of the will of Edward I's Queen, Eleanor of Castile.

The early medieval populace of Berwick would be native Scots, men of Lothian, Northumbrians, Scandinavians and Cumbrians and folk from Flanders, the Rhineland, Northern France and England. Contemporary documents speak of the ships of these people carrying on trade at Berwick. The *Orkneyinga Saga*, for instance, tells a story of a wealthy merchant Knut who 'spent much of his time at Berwick' in the mid-twelfth century, and recounts how he was robbed during a raid on Berwick by Earl Erland and Swein.

The chronicler William of Newburgh confirms that David had some control of the east coast as far as the Tees. Ecclesiastically Berwick was in the archdeaconry of Lothian and in the diocese of St Andrews up to 1310, after which it was in the See of Durham. And it was to become an increasingly valuable source of income for both king and church. The customs duties from imports went direct to the king, and grants of fishing rights and rents from royal demesne estates, through the king, helped fund the religious houses. At this time Berwick was importing textiles, with the materials to process them, alum, woad and teasels, and was exporting foodstuffs, wool, felt, hides, skins and livestock.

When Henry I of England died in 1135 his daughter Matilda (David I's niece) was nominated to the throne but was opposed by her cousin Stephen. David invaded England four times in

Matilda's interest and laid waste to Northumberland. David's army, a motley host of Scots, Norwegians, English and 'those bestial men', as Richard of Hexham called them, the Picts of Galloway, perpetrated unspeakable horrors. Although Bamburgh held out against him, David made ground, but on 22 August 1138 at Cowton Moor, near Northallerton, he lost the Battle of the Standard. Yet, diplomatically he did well: he won the old earldom of Northumberland for his son Henry in 1139.

King David I died in 1153 at Carlisle 'in an attitude of devotion' and was succeeded by his grandson Malcolm IV, nicknamed 'the maiden' for his virginity—Henry, Earl of Northumberland, had died the year before. The youth of Malcolm—he was eleven when he succeeded—led to more jockeyings for control, and the new King of England, Henry II (1154-89), stormed across the country recovering properties lost in Stephen's reign. Bamburgh was restored to him and in 1157 Malcolm paid a kind of homage to Henry at Chester. On Malcolm's death in 1165 Berwick was to enter a new historical phase.

CHAPTER 2

Berwick Guilds, Castle and Royal Mint

Berwick castle is first mentioned with any certainty in 1163 during the reign of Malcolm IV, by the chronicler Reginald of Durham, although in 1127 the monk Edward of Coldingham, in the *Liber Vitae Ecclesiae Dunelmensis*, had mentioned that David I was asking for wood for his 'pile' at Berwick, which would suggest supplies for castle wall repairs. Even so, by the twelfth century Berwick castle was hardly more than a palisaded site, and in the early days the castle stood outwith the burgh and formed no part of it. In 1174 William I of Scotland, nicknamed 'The Lion', was hellbent on recovering what Malcolm IV had lost to Henry II of England and allied himself with the rebellious sons of Henry; thus supported, he descended confidently on Alnwick. Here William was captured, and by the Treaty of Falaise, Berwick fell to the English along with Stirling, Edinburgh, Roxburgh and Jedburgh. By the end of the twelfth century Henry II was enlarging and strengthening the castle along Norman lines with stone replacing some of the woodwork—the castle and burgh had been burned in the campaign of 1174, we are confidently told by the *Gesta Henrici Secundi*, and Jordan Fantosme, in *Chronicle of Stephen &c*, relates how Berwick was burned by the English Justiciar, Richard de Lucy, and the Constable, Humphrey de Bohan. During this period Berwick castle would have a motte with a ditch—a palisaded bank enclosing a wooden tower; the whole would be a wooden improvised fortress until Henry II exchanged it for stonework. The early buildings of the castle would include a chapel, a smithy, stables and garrison quarters. From around 1124, when Berwick had a sheriff (*Vicecomes de Berwic*), he and his entourage would be semi-permanent residents of the castle. The sheriff's function at this time would be that of chief legal officer under the king.

From its first existence the castle was the focal point in a political sense, whereas the town was not so until much later. The castle remained a strategic pawn, and it was not until the thirteenth century that the Warden of the town was in any sense 'on a par' with the castle's Constable, the former deputising in certain cases when the latter was away. Up to the early sixteenth century the town and castle were always mentioned individually. From the castle, too, the sheriff carried out his military duties and civil administration, raising taxes and keeping records.

A portion of the taxes—like Henry II's *wardmonies*—went to pay for professional soldiers, thus releasing the burgesses and tenantry of Berwick's policies from duty as castle guards. Among the sheriff's entourage would be porters, stewards, cooks, brewers, bakers, servers, grooms, herdsmen, seamstresses and so on, along with carpenters, masons, smiths and labourers. In time of peace the soldiery probably numbered only some fifty at Berwick castle. It is interesting to note in the King's Remembrancer Accounts of 1302 that archers were also employed as masons and carpenters at Berwick, receiving extra pay (2d) for such duties. The earliest governor of Berwick castle to be mentioned was Gaufridus de Nevile in the *Chartulary of Melrose* (1174) which records for the king, *Tempore quo Gufridus de Neiville habuit custodiam castelli mei de Berwic* (At which time Gaufridus de Nevile lived as the governor of my castle at Berwick).

The castle was regular host to the officers of the Scottish king's court which was formed on two levels, hereditary and non-hereditary. So the king's Scottish court at Berwick castle would include a *dapifer*, or steward, who supervised the king's hall and household personnel; a constable, to command the king's knights; a marischal or two, to assist the constable, and a butler to provide a good table. All of these were hereditary positions. The non-hereditary ones included a chancellor, who supervised the court chaplains and chapel where the great seal was kept (which authenticated documents in an illiterate age), and a chamberlain who acted largely as the king's domestic treasurer.

In 1189 Berwick castle was sold back to William by Richard I who was trying to raise the wind for his crusade. During the period 1109 to 1214 there was an epoch of 'armed friendship' between William the Lion and the new king of England, John Lackland. William died at Stirling in December 1214 and was succeeded by his son Alexander II who led his nation into a 'golden age' with a great building of cathedrals and parish churches; this was a period when an established pattern of streets had emerged at Berwick. The earliest recorded street occupation of Berwick town is around 1200 along the line of (Saint) Marygate; and towards the Tweed from the top of Hide Hill and Woolmarket to Ravensdowne. The earliest streets mentioned are: *Briggate*(modern Bridge Street and Love Lane), closely associated with the waterfront commercial properties; *Butcher Street* (at the corner of Church Street and Marygate); *Church Street*, by 1227; *Cowgate* (a track to the Snook, past the site of Holy Trinity Churchyard); *Land of Dodyn* (Eastern Lane area); *Foulford*; *Narougate* (Eastern Lane); *The Ness* (where the abbey of Newbattle had land next to the 'great houses of Melrose'); and *Land of Walef* (West Street).

In England on 15 June 1215 King John met his barons at Runnymede and put his great seal to the charter we know as Magna Carta. John's difficulties with his nobles rekindled Scotland's ambitions to secure Cumberland, Westmorland and Northumberland, and Alexander allied himself with John's enemies. John retaliated and Berwick, Roxburgh, Coldingham, Dunbar and Haddington were all attacked. Walter of Coventry in his *Memoriale* noted John's harrying of Berwick and his indiscriminate torture of men and women. The *Chronica de Mailros* also records how King John 'brought Jews with him there, and . . . . made them directors of [this] wickedness'.

King John died in October 1216 and was succeeded by nine-year-old Henry III with whom Alexander II became reconciled. Referring again to the chronicle of the monks of Melrose, we see that on the Kalends (the 1st) of December 1217, Alexander, who had invaded England, the realm of the Pope's ally King John, was absolved within Berwick castle of his excommunication by the Pope represented by the Archbishop

The Constable Tower, Berwick Castle, set in today's Castle Vale Park, within the grounds of the Abbeyfield Society Home. The tower, with its fragment of curtain wall, dates from the late thirteenth or early fourteenth century and formed a section of the southeast portion of the castle. Constable Tower retains its medieval garderobe (privy) and fish-tail arrow slits (*Neil Potts*).

of York and the Bishop of Durham. The Anglo-Scottish reconciliation was to last through the reign and was sealed by nuptial alliance. Alexander married Joan, daughter of King John, in 1221 and in 1235 Alexander's sister Marjorie married Gilbert, Earl of Pembroke, the Earl Marshall, on the day of St Peter ad Vincula (1 Aug) in the chapel at Berwick castle. By the Treaty of York in 1237 the longstanding dispute over the frontier with England was finally settled with the Scots agreeing to surrender their claim to the three northern counties.

Alexander II got on with enforcing the rule of law at home and is known to have dated several of his charters from his castle at Berwick which would be deemed the king's personal property. These charters would be sealed by the great seal of Scotland which travelled with the king and was kept in his chapel at Berwick on his visits there. Round about this time too

seals associated with Berwick first appeared. While discussing
the seals of the medieval burgh of Berwick in 1917 (*History of the
Berwick Naturalists' Club, 1919*), C.H.Hunter Blair notes that the
earliest known seal of the town is on a convention document
between one 'H' (either Henry of Silton, circa 1253-58, or
Henry of Horncastle, circa 1266-79), prior of Coldingham, and
the mayor of the burgh; within the charter the seal is described
as *sigillum commune*. The rough and ready seal shows a bear
standing in front of a three-branched tree (trad: wych elm) and
Lombardic type with SIG [ILLUM COMMUNITATIS VILLE
B] VRGENSIVM [SUPER TUEDAM] (Seal of the Commonalty
of the Town of Berwick-upon-Tweed).

Another seal discovered in 1917 showed a gowned man, with
a bear with a cord round its neck; on the bear's body are the
three leopards of England, all surmounted by a fragment of the
banner of England. It is likely that this seal, attached to a
document dated 1 November 1315, was made some time after
the capture of Berwick by Edward I in 1296. Hunter Blair also
describes another three-inch seal of the burgh used in
documents dated 1330 and 1342; the obverse shows a passant
chained bear with a tree containing two branches, while on the
reverse is the Holy Trinity, a probable allusion to the parish
church. The style dates from the capture of the town by Bruce in
April 1318. Hunter Blair then describes a 1¾-inch fifteenth-
century seal with a bear beneath a tree between two shields of
France and England with a design of Our Lord in Glory and the
legend: SIGILLV MAIORATVS VILLA BERWICI SUPER
TWEDAM (Seal of the Mayor of the Town of Berwick-upon-
Tweed). The seal was used up to the nineteenth century with the
rebus of a bear and wych-elm for Berwick (see page 199). The
British Museum also catalogues seals used by Edward I,
Edward II, Edward III and Henry IV for documents relative to
their 'lands beyond Tweed'. Edward I's shows a bear and tree
on the obverse with a sixfoiled panel and: SIGILLV[M]
D[OMIN]I EDWARDI DEI GRA [TIA] REX ANGLIE PRO
TERRA SVA ULTRA TWEDAM (Seal of Lord Edward, by the
Grace of God King of England, for his lands beyond the Tweed).

The reverse shows the shield of England hanging from a tree with EDWARDVS DEI GRATIA REX ANGLIE DOMINVS HIBERNIE ET DUX ACQUITAINIE (Edward, by the Grace of God, Lord of Ireland and Duke of Aquitaine). The treasury at Durham cathedral holds a one-inch seal which was used by the Chamberlain of Berwick; it was affixed to a document dated 20 October 1365 and was used by William de la Vale described as *camerarius [chamberlain] villae Berwici super Twedam* in the document, and who identified the seal as *sigillum oficii mei camerarii* (official seal of my chamberlain). The seal shows the banner of England with a tree on each side and a bear, and is probably at least thirty years older than the document.

All of this shows Berwick's increased importance from the thirteenth century, and round about this time too Berwick's guilds were developing. Indeed guilds existed in Berwick from the early days of commerce, as craftsmen of each trade met at their own 'feasts' to form trade associations. The earliest trade associations in Berwick were those of the baxters (bakers), the fleshers (butchers) and the salmon fishers. These guilds took real form in the reign of David I of Scotland, and the laws governing trade in Berwick were codified in 1249, wherein the different guilds were amalgamated into one. In those days the governance of commerce was in the hands of the guildsmen and the town administration was in the hands of the military.

The guildsmen met in their separate groups in the halls owned by the friars, or in the friary chapels themselves. We know for a fact that guildsmen were meeting in the hall of the Trinitarians at Berwick in 1248 and probably endowed altars in the various chapels. For instance an altar may have been set up to St Crispin the Martyr (feast day, 25 October) by the shoemakers, or to St Bartholomew the Apostle (feast day, 24 August), the patron of the fleshers. Probably the greatest of the 'halls' in Berwick was the Red Hall of the Flemings. Certainly it is the most frequently mentioned and was a fortified factory with its own palisading and trench. It would have had two or three inner courts smeared with red paint as was the custom of the Low Countries.

From their halls the guildsmen regulated their trade, and by 1283 this ranged from wool and hides to the seasonal prices of ale and mutton, and the sale of fish, hay, oats, cheese, butter, hemp, leather and corn. The guildsmen enforced a strict rule excluding lepers from the burgh. If a leper entered, he was stripped naked, his clothes were burned and he was driven from the gates of Berwick by the burgh sergeant. The guildsmen operated a scheme by which those duped by traders (for example, keeping the best apples at the front of their stalls and selling the diseased ones from the back) were compensated, and 'engrossing' was prevented; this meant that 'no burgess shall have more than any one buyer of wool making purchases on his behalf'. Other rules were that burghers could not trade for animals outwith certain times, all seaborne foods had to be carried away by sunset, and no married woman might buy wool.

Berwick's trade practices were governed by the Statutes of the Guild (*Statutae Gildae*) up to James VI's charter of 1603, and thereafter to the Municipal Corporation Act of 1835. Indeed this meant that from 1603 the guildsmen took over the governance of the town with the powers of a Town Council until the 1835 Act. The earliest record of a guild meeting in Berwick is October 1506.

So Berwick's town seal and guilds were established by the time that Alexander II died of fever in 1249 during a punitive expedition to the West of Scotland. He was succeeded by his son the seven-year old Alexander III.

By the Treaty of Perth in 1266 Alexander III extended his kingdom with the acquisition of the Isle of Man and the Hebrides and the king celebrated his birthday during September at Berwick castle, the good wishes of England being conveyed in the person of Prince Edmund, Earl of Lancaster. In 1268 John, son of John Comyn, was knighted at Berwick by Alexander III (John was the father of the Red Comyn slain by Bruce). In 1278 the Scots king was wrangling at Berwick with the Bishop of Durham about the Marches: in the Middle Ages the area north of Berwick was known to most as the East March.

It is fitting at this point to sketch in the relevance of Berwick castle itself. After it had been strengthened by Henry II, who lost it to the Scots, we shall see that Edward I recaptured the castle and the town in 1296. The existing fortifications of the castle were strengthened by a ditch, bank and wooden palisade. This wooden defence was replaced by a stone wall during 1297-98. The remaining walls of the castle today—the White Wall (Breakneck Steps)—running down from the station site to the Tweed probably date from this time too. We learn that in 1303 the gate defences were improved. Throughout the Middle Ages the castle was quite separate from the town and there is no real evidence that the town developed because of the importance of the castle.

During the siege of 1318 the castle walls were found to be so low that archdeacon John Barbour is able to tell us in his poem *The Brus* that the defenders were only a spear's thrust from the ground, so the walls were raised. Records show too that Berwick castle was designed as the administrative base for Edward I's Anglo-Scottish campaigns and was the office of a chamberlain whose duties included surveying the king's Scottish castles with a clerk to monitor Berwick's fabric. By Edward III's reign the two jobs had been combined in one man, Walter of Weston. Berwick castle too was a centre for the manufacture and storage of the king's siege engines.

Berwick's medieval castle consisted of a curtain wall, with a single main entrance where the station forecourt is now located. The curtain wall had ten known towers around its perimeter exclusive of the strong detached defensive tower on the entrance bridge wall called the Percy Tower by the English and the Douglas Tower by the Scots; this was built around 1303. To enter the castle in medieval times one had to pass through the town wall and the barbican and drawbridge of the Douglas Tower, then cross three main drawbridges to reach the fortified donjon main gate. The linking causeway here was still to be seen in 1846.

The town had its own gateway, St Mary Gate, somewhere near the junction of Castle Terrace and Northumberland

Avenue today, which spanned the road into Scotland. The wall
of the castle facing the town was always given special attention
for fortification in case the town fell into unfriendly hands.
Even so the castle stood at a disadvantageously lower level than
the town.

The domestic buildings within the castle were mainly ranged
against the south and west walls. The inventory of 1292 defines
a few of the domestic buildings: a larder, a kitchen, a buttery, a
wardrobe and a smith's forge. In 1951 the Hall and Captain's
Lodgings were identified by the Buttress Tower and the White
Wall. Today the station platforms occupy the site of the castle's
Great Hall. In modern Castle Vale Park (within the private
grounds of the Abbeyfield Home) is to be found a fragment of a
curtain wall and the polygonal Constable Tower of the late
thirteenth century. This tower with its fishtail arrow slits and
garderobe was the south-east corner of the castle. The other
main towers of the castle were the Postern Tower, the Chapel
Tower, the Buttress Tower, the Water Tower, two Gun Towers,
the Barmkin Tower (defending an iron postern), the Bakehouse
Tower, the Bonkill Tower (the Granary Tower) and the
Gunners' Tower (the Armoury). Probably from the fifteenth
century Berwick castle would be defended with such guns as
sakers, falcons and hagbuts.

The castle walls were pierced by a number of postern gates 'to
issue into the fields' as the Court Rolls have it. To the north the
town and castle were protected by an 80ft wide and 40ft deep
ditch fortified by a palisade, and this is identified for us by the
chronicler Walter of Guisborne.

These days the castle walls are best viewed from Coronation
Park and Tommy the Miller's Field, and their full extent may be
seen, although the ashlar facing has vanished. The tallest piece
of extant wall was probably the Bakehouse Tower, and the
sixteenth-century semi-circular Gunners' Tower commands
the north shore of the Tweed. The White Wall of 1297-98 was
constructed to stop an enemy bypassing the castle and attacking
the town or reinforcing any attack from the river. These walls
lead down to the heavily fortified Water Tower commenced in

The White Wall, 1297-98, of the castle descends from the heights to the River Tweed. The wall was built by Edward I to stop an enemy skirting the castle to attack the town. The stairs protected by the wall are called the Breakneck Steps. When the railway station was being constructed above, navvys uncovered a large quantity of human skeletons by the White Wall (*Neil Potts*).

1539. The path and steps of today's Castle Vale Park follow the course of a stream which flowed down the castle's east side; the stream powered the town's mills set to the north of the castle from medieval times. A dam was built in the thirteenth century to the north of the present line of the Great North Road and it held back vital water supplies; the expanse of water, drained by the railway constructors to make room for sidings and sheds, was known as the Tapee Lake.

Berwick castle was one of the fortifications surveyed by John Cutte and Richard Gouge in 1488 as a part of their assessment of the northern castles for Henry VII. Their recommendations led to the 'scouring' of the castle's inner and outer ditches and the keeping 'playne and without house, hille or diche' the area known as the Greenses.

By 1536 most of the walls and towers had been reconstructed to house, fire and withstand artillery, and in 1542 the new White Wall Tower was complete. In 1558 it was proposed to demolish the castle, but it survived until 1604 when it was granted to Sir George Hume by James VI & I. Hume, later Earl of Dunbar, set about building a tower house within the castle walls and it was almost complete when he died in 1611. All work ceased and the castle, the house and the walls became a quarry for various building projects in the town like the parish church and the barracks. In the eighteenth century the south walls collapsed, and by Victoria's day it was in a very fragmentary state. In those days the castle walls facing the town enclosed only a field in which was sited a windmill.

The castle passed to the family of the Earl of Suffolk and down the centuries there were various lessees of the castle grounds, corns mills and windmill. For instance the Earl of Suffolk sold the castle to Berwick Corporation for £320 in 1641 and it was used as a source of wood, stone and lead. In the 1790s the title of the castle area fell to the Askew family of Castlehills. It was with the Askew family that the North British Railway Company negotiated in 1843 for the site of their new railway link. In 1844 a Bill was passed in Parliament for the making of the railway from Berwick to Edinburgh, and in 1846 the railway opened, thus effectively destroying the castle site. During the excavations for the railway, piles of human bones were found to the left of the White Walls.

Berwick castle was the location of the royal mint at Berwick as it was the safest place to keep the punches, dies and precious metals. The first Scottish king to issue his own independent coinage was David I, although up to the twelfth century a wide range of continental, Northumbrian and English coins would have circulated in Berwick for commerce. The early sterlings of David were based on the coin patterns of King Stephen of England and are dated after 1135.

The early Berwick coins were first struck as blanks from sheets of silver; the blanks were then clipped to the correct weight and passed on to the striker who stamped out the coins with his standard dies with obverse and reverse patterns, and so the coins were known as hammered issues. The moneymaking team, the silver melter and sheet hammerer, a blank cutter and a striker, were led by a mint master whose name appeared on the reverse of the coins. Thus early examples have the Latin inscription FOLPAT ON BERV[IC]I for 'Folpat the moneyer at Berwick'. David I's coins from Berwick showed the king's bust and his name in Latin: DAVIT REX CSOCIE (ie, SCOTIE) for 'David, King of Scotland'.

William I (1165-1214) also had pennies struck for him at Berwick by moneyers William and Adam which were very similar to David's with crowned bust and sceptre and WIL[LEL]MVS REX, but it is possible that when the castle and town were in English hands during 1174-86 no coins were struck at Berwick at all. Minting was resumed in 1195, according to the *Chronicle of Melrose*.

Alexander II, from 1214, was the next Scottish king to have coins struck at Berwick with known pennies issued by the moneyers WALE (Walter) and ROB (Robert) working in conjunction. Alexander III, from 1249, had a much wider known range of coins struck at Berwick, some with a beardless head, squarish face, crowned, or variations with ALEXANDER REX SCOTORVM. It is probable that, by the thirteenth century, Berwick was supplying most of Scotland's small change.

Edward I's puppet, John Balliol, also had Berwick as his main mint for pennies and halfpennies, with IOHANNES DEI GRA[TIA] REX SCOTORVM and the motto SALVUM FAC POPVLVM TVVM DOMINE ('O Lord save Thy People' from *Psalm* xxviii.9). In 1296 Edward I made Berwick a financial centre (ie, an Exchequer) as important as Westminster. One of his earliest financial officers at Berwick was Hugh de Cressingham, King's Treasurer. The Berwick coins of the Scottish kings circulated long after their deaths; Alexander II's, for instance, were used right up to the reign of Robert I the Bruce (ie, 1306-29).

During Edward I's reign Berwick, seemingly quite independent from the Royal Mint at London, made its own punches and dies, the bulk of the money probably being issued for two main, local, purposes: the payment of troops, and commerce.

At Berwick Edward I struck pennies, halfpennies and farthings, with the following typical inscriptions:

1d. EDWARANGLDNShYB VILL/ ABE/REV/VICI
(*Edwardus Rex Anglorum Dominus Hiberniae*)
'Edward, King of England and Lord of Ireland'.
½d. EDW ARTANGLDNShB VILL/LAB/ERE/WIC
¼d. ED . . . . REX VIL/ . . . ./ERV/VICI.

Edward II continued the mint at Berwick and appointed one Radulphus Sutton as Controller of the Customs and of the mint. In 1311-12 Roger de Goswyk was keeper of the King's Mint at Berwick (the profits on the issues of this year produced £19.18s.0d reckoned at 4d a pound) to be succeeded during 1312-15 by Robert de Walkington and Nicholas de Acton. The first coins from Berwick ascribed to Edward II are easily identified and dated (for the first and last time), for they correspond with the issues of the English mint. Edward II issued pennies of silver at Berwick very similar in inscription to those of Edward I, but the later issues somewhat deteriorated in craftsmanship, differing in size one from another and figuring

Dominated by the Victorian Royal Border Bridge, the castle's ruined Water Tower dates from 1539-42, and protected the fortification's own landing-place. The tower was heavily fortified with guns to rake the lower reaches of the river. From the Water Tower, it is said, a huge chain stretched across the River Tweed to the opposite shore to prevent enemy ships from proceeding upriver (*Neil Potts*).

off-centre. It is probable that during this period the punches for the dies (but not the dies themselves) came to Berwick from London.

When the Scots lost Berwick to the English in 1333 (the semi-Scottish mint continued from 1318-33 as probably the English left their punches behind on evacuation), Edward III lost no time in operating a mint there with one John de Bourdon as Chamberlain. Giving his account from Michaelmas 1333 to 24 June 1334, the Chamberlain included among his receipts: 'From the moneyers for licence to coin money in Berwick 13s. 4d.' Profits rose to 22s.2¾d by 1336 but in the accounts of Robert de Emeldon, Chamberlain in 1341, there is a note of '7s.6d received from a moneyer making halfpence and farthings at Berwick, to wit upon £22.10s.0d struck and minted in the port and vill of Berwick into halfpence and farthings to wit for every li (£)4d.'

From 1333 the coinage of Berwick was on a small scale, mostly halfpence and farthings, bearing the double bear's head in one/two quarters of the reverse instead of the usual three pellets. The bear's head makes them firmly Berwick issues.

Edward III's coins had a little more ambitious lettering; for instance his farthings read:
EWARDVS DEI GRA[*TIA*] VIL/L BER/VICI
with bear's head in quarters 1 & 3.

The heyday of Berwick coins was undoubtedly during the reigns of the three Edwards, with some issues being extant up to 1461-82. When Berwick was in the hands of James III (1460-88) of Scotland, he appears to have coined to a considerable extent in the town. On the reverse of some of his groats and half-groats is seen a mullet in each quarter of the cross and in the inner circle VILLA BERWICI: the legend on the obverse being, JACOBVS D[EI] GRA [TIA] RE [X] SCOTOR [VM] and on the reverse: D [OMI] N [V] S P [RO] TECTOR M [EV] S ET LIB [E] R [A] T [O] R [MEVS], which may be translated:'God is my defender and my redeemer'. The abbreviations of the mint name are: BE, BER, BEREWIC, BERV, BERVI, BERWIH, VILLA BERWICI and VILLA BERWICHI.

An Act of Parliament of King James IV (1488-1513) mentions groats struck by one Gilbert Fish which were to be commonly called 'Berwick groats'. But as Berwick had been firmly in the hands of the English for years before that, the groats had not been struck at Berwick. During an excavation at Aberdeen in 1886 a treasure trove was found by workmen of 12,267 coins among which 220 were Berwick coins. The latter were shared out amongst authorities and institutions.

Berwick was the principal mint of medieval Scotland and the dies of the burgh were often interchanged with other mints. For instance when the Perth mint was re-opened after Alexander II it is likely that Berwick dies were used to start them off. When Berwick was returned to Scotland in 1461 the series of coins of James III were restruck using Edinburgh dies.

By Alexander III's time Berwick had won far-flung fame and the description of the burgh as 'a second Alexandria' was on the lips of commentators. In 1286 the customs at Berwick were said to be worth £2190. By this year too a road to Kelso from Berwick had been established, and it continued across Scotland to Lesmahagow. It was a time of increased sophistication in lifestyle, architecture and learning, but it was a prelude to disaster. Alexander's immediate heirs all died and one stormy night in 1286 the king himself plunged to his death over the cliffs at Pettycur Bay, Fife. Berwick was to suffer greatly as a direct consequence.

CHAPTER THREE

Berwick's Medieval Religious Houses and Parish Churches

The medieval religious houses in Berwick comprised friaries, hospitals and a nunnery; there were no abbeys within the burgh, although the presence of monks would be constant throughout the Middle Ages as many of the great Scottish monasteries owned properties in the town. The religious houses flourished in Berwick from 1230 when the town was indisputably Scottish and situated within the diocese of St Andrews; but when the English held the town in 1333, Edward III ordered that the Scottish friars be removed from their houses there.

Within the history of monasticism in Scotland, Berwick is a lateish arrival, for it was with the marriage of Edmund Ironside's granddaughter Margaret to Malcolm III in 1069 that medieval monasticism was introduced to the northern kingdom; remembering, of course too, that a monastic rule obtained at Iona from 563. Monastic influence was known in Berwick before the opening of the first religious house around 1153, for the Benedictines had been settled in their priory at Coldingham by around 1139, and from 1128 the monks of the Order of Tiron were at Kelso, and both houses had interests in Berwick.

It was indeed the processing of monastic goods and supplies that gave Berwick its first commercial boost. A colony of Flemings established their place of business at the Red Hall, and they exported most of the monastic produce to the staple at Bruges. The Red Hall, incidentally, is placed by tradition in the Woolmarket, but it is likelier that it was closer to the waterfront near the south-east end of modern Bridge Street. During March 1296 this hall was burned down by the soldiers of Edward I.

The earliest recorded religious house in Berwick, and indeed the earliest Cistercian nunnery in Scotland, was founded around 1153 as a representative of by far the most prominent order in Scotland. The Cistercian Order had been founded at Citeaux in France in 1098. It had come to England in 1128 and the Berwick sisters were known as the White Nuns, because of the colour of their habits. Their church and domestic buildings were sited by tradition at Halyston, Halidon Hill, and are recorded as being at South Berwick, the medieval way of distinguishing the burgh from North Berwick in East Lothian. The actual site of their house was probably in the area near the top of modern Castle Terrace where it makes a junction with the road to Duns (indeed it is thought that Meadowhill House was built in part from stones from the nunnery). The house was dedicated to the Blessed Virgin and St Leonard, the one-time hermit and patron saint of prisoners. After the conventual church and buildings were largely wasted during the action of the battle of Halidon Hill, a grant was made to the nuns by Edward III to repair their nunnery. It is likely that the royal largesse was a consequence of the nuns having tended to the wounded after the bloody battle. But it seems that the nunnery never really recovered from the war damage.

In 1390-1 there were only two nuns left and the possessions and lands were granted to the Abbey of the Premonstratensian Canons at Dryburgh. It is likely too that the two nuns went to the Cistercian nunnery of St Bothan's (modern site, Abbey St Bathans, Berwickshire). The *Calendar of Scottish Supplications to Rome, 1418-22* records that there were scarcely any traces of the nunnery left by 1420. Some historians suggest that a second nunnery was extant in Berwick, but this might have been a cell of St Leonards. The whole picture is unclear.

As with their Cistercian brothers in the town, the nuns at the house at Halystone were dedicated to hard work. Their chapel would be simple with no riches and ornamentation and they would be unlikely to employ servants. The house would be run as a priory with the senior nun acting as Mother Prioress. An important part of their daily tasks would be the spinning and weaving of wool and linen for their own clothes and some

embroidery for church garments and tapestries. There would
be some teaching of little children within the sisters' cloisters.
The nuns would probably take in women guests as lodgers,
pilgrims perhaps on their way to and from the shrines at
Dunfermline, St Andrews and Durham. And it is believed that
they brought up the orphaned daughters of Guild members
(see page 145); some charitable work amongst the poor in the
burgh would also be undertaken.

The bulk of the religious houses at Berwick were friaries. The
friars of Berwick were strictly not monks at all, but mendicant
brothers under a resident, or semi-resident, prior. They
worked amongst the laity as priests and instructors. Their
properties in the burgh would be held in trust by individual
burgesses, or a group thereof, as it was against the principles of
the friars to invest in land and draw rents or tithes; it is likely,
though, that their gardens and smallholdings within the burgh
would be deemed to be their possessions.

The friars conducted daily services, preached sermons
within their chapels and on the streets, buried the dead, tended
the poor and sick, and looked after the interests of their Orders.
The friaries in Berwick would almost all be single-storied with
churches divided by a small tower into choir and nave. The
choir was reserved for the friars with stalls, altar and square-cut
east end. The people would kneel in the nave during Divine
Office. The friars were sworn to poverty and their buildings
would be of the simplest; the cloisters and other conventual
buildings would be of haphazard plan, particularly those of the
Dominicans who had no fixed architectural rule of thumb.

The actual daily timetable of the nuns and friars in Berwick
would vary from summer to winter, and there would be some
variation between the Orders. The friars'/nuns' day would
begin around 2.00 am and went on until around 6.30 pm in the
winter and 8.00 pm in summer, and the day would be divided
by the eight services of the church. Matins, Lauds and Prime
took place (generally) before daybreak; Tierce, Sext and None
occurred during the day; and the last two, Vespers and
Compline, were at sunset and just before retiring. The Mass

would follow Tierce and this would be a service to which the laity would especially attend. The friars would spend less time in reading and meditation than their monkish brothers.

The oldest friary in Berwick was the house which Alexander II is thought to have founded in 1231 for the Franciscan Friars Minor, known as the Grey Friars. This was the year when the Friars Minor are believed to have entered Scotland. The *Pontificale Scoticanum* tells us their church was dedicated by David de Bernham, Bishop of St Andrews, on 6 May 1244. David de Bernham, incidentally, was born at Berwick and was of an ancient family of burgesses who supplied at least one mayor of the town; he died at Nenthorn in 1253 and was buried at Kelso Abbey.

The Franciscans were dedicated to absolute poverty and they lived on alms. They usually possessed one habit only, a girdle of cord and one pair of breeches; they wore no shoes. At first the friars were very popular in Berwick, but their support waned, especially when they started to use professional beggars (procurators) and amass monies. In particular too there was rivalry between Franciscans and Dominicans about their 'begging areas'. Some of the friars (called limitors) bought the sole rights of the local order to beg, hoping to make a profit.

Edward III ordered the Scottish Franciscans to be replaced by English friars in 1333. It has been suggested that he suspected that the Scottish friars 'spied' for Scotland during the disturbances. Nothing much is known of the friary after a grant from the English Exchequer was made in 1337.

There would be up to a maximum of thirty Franciscan friars in Berwick at any one time, but the number fluctuated. The site of their house is likely to have been near the north stretch of the Edwardian walls near the Bell Tower, the buildings probably comprising a chapel and primitive living quarters. A cruciform gravestone was found hereabouts in the lane near the tower and may have been from the priory cemetery. Several Berwick Franciscans rose to high office: John of Berwick was regent at Oxford; Richard of Durham was one of the writers of Lanercost Priory, Cumbria— he was confessor to Devorguilla, the wife of

John Balliol, and in the *Chronica de Lanercost* ascribed the decline
of Berwick to the burgesses not giving generously to the
Franciscan funds; and the Franciscan philosopher John Duns
Scotus (c.1260-1305) must have known the house. Indeed John
Duns Scotus's uncle, the Franciscan Minister General, Elias
Duns, had placed Berwick firmly in the Scottish province of the
order; after his 'fall' in 1239 it was allocated to the Province
Minister at Newcastle. The Berwick friars always rankled at this
and thought themselves Scottish; after 1329 they became an
autonomous vicariate. There are a few known guardians
(Wardens) of the Berwick Franciscans; in 1291, William de
Blakeden; and in 1318, Adam Newton—who acted as
ambassador for Cardinals Gaucelin and Luke, to carry letters to
Richard I.

The keen rivals of the Franciscans, the Dominicans, were the
next to have a house founded in Berwick by Alexander II
around 1240, dedicated to St Peter Martyr of Milan. Known as
the Black Friars, the Dominicans appeared in Scotland in 1230
and were not as extreme in their poverty as the Franciscans.
They individually possessed a coat, three tunics and shoes.
Their habit of a white robe, scapular, cowl and black open
mantle made them prominent figures in the Berwick streets.
Dominicans were usually well-educated at their mother house
and consequently they were great teachers.

Incidentally we know that there were (monastic) schools in
Berwick long before 1279 when the 'rector of the school of
South Berwick' was a commissary (an agent) of Radulphus de
Greenlaw, Abbot of Dunfermline—the rector's work would be
to act as link-man between the abbey and its churches at
Foulden and Lamberton.

The duties of the Dominicans included prayer, the
suppression of heresy and the spread of Gospel truth. Their
first chapel in Berwick is thought to have been close by the
castle, near to where Castlegate meets High Greens, and in this
sanctified place Edward I held discussion to debate the claims
of the magnates in 1291. It is noted in the *Calendar of Entries in the
Papal Registers* (1893) that in 1285 the Pope allowed Walter

Frazer, Bishop of St Andrews, to sell to the Dominicans that property in Berwick which had belonged to the Friars of Penitence. It appears that the Friars of the Penitence of Jesus Christ (also known as the Friars of the Sack) had had a house within the 'parish of Holy Trinity of South Berwick' founded in 1267 by the agreement of Roger Prior of Coldingham; the order was suppressed in 1274. This new property of the Dominicans was sited near Love Lane. As with the Franciscans, the Berwick Dominicans were removed by the order of Edward III and supplanted by English Dominicans. The later history of the Dominicans at Berwick is obscure, but they are thought to have moved to a site at Ravensdale (near Love Lane) around 1290.

The house of the Carmelite friars—the Brothers of the Blessed Virgin Mary of Mount Carmel, Palestine—is said to have been founded in 1270 by Sir John Gray, who may have had a hand in the founding of the Franciscan house too. Like the other friars' houses in Berwick, the Carmelites would receive grants and gifts from 'the fermes of Berwick' as well as royal purses. As a part of their duties the Carmelites took care of the chapel, with its altar dedicated to St Thomas the Martyr of Canterbury, within the king's apartments at Berwick Castle, and administered a chapel dedicated to the Holy Trinity on the Berwick Bridge destroyed by flood in 1294. It is probable that their house was set within the Ness near Palace Street. The activities of the Carmelites in Berwick are obscure after the recorded payments from the English Exchequer in 1337.

The friars of the order of Hermits of St Augustine—the Augustinians—had only one house in Scotland and it was at Berwick. It is thought to have been founded around 1329. They were replaced in 1337, as had been the other orders. Details about this house are very sparse and confusing but the last mention of the Augustinians in court records is in 1406 when they gave a loan of 26s 8d to Holy Island Priory. Some authorities say that these friars were of the Segden Hermitage some two miles north-west of Berwick, but this is unclear.

Records show that the Trinitarians—the order of the Most Holy Trinity for the Redemption of Captives, dedicated to raise funds to ransom Christian pilgrims held captive in Islamic lands—had one house at Berwick on Dominican land and their church was long called the 'Chapel of Ravendale' (from 1289 to 1539). In Elizabethan times the medieval chapel was used as a storehouse (north side of Love Lane), the site of a later granary. The Trinitarians were not mendicants but canons, and their Berwick house was founded some time before 1240-48; about 1248 they were given custody of a new house at Dunbar. The brothers had charge of the hospital of St Edward at Berwick (see page 37), and by 1447 the house was non-conventual and its ministry was transferred to Coupar Angus in 1456. Some time before 1488, James III granted the revenues of the Berwick Trinitarians to its brother house of the Holy Cross at Peebles.

The priest-poet William Dunbar (c.1460-1514), one of the commissioners in the negotiations of the marriage between James IV and Margaret Tudor, the most 'polished' of the early Scottish poets, and probably himself a Franciscan, is credited with writing the poem 'The Freiris of Berwik'. In the poem he specifies four orders (there were five) and particularly mentions the Carmelites, the Friars Minor and the Dominicans. Here is an extract from the *Bannatyne MS* (1568):

As it befell, and happinnit in to deid
Upoun a revir, the quhilk is callid Tweid.
At Tweidis mouth there stands a noble town,
Where many lords have been of great renown:
Where many a lady als been, fair of face,
And many ane fresh lusty gallant was.
Into this town the quhilk is callit Berwik—
Upon the sea, there standis none it like;
For it is walled well about with stane,
And double *stankis* castin many ane,   ditches
And syne the castel is so strong and wight,
With statelie towers, and turrets high on hicht,
With *kirnalis* wrought craftilie with all;   crenelles
The portcullis most subtely to fall,
When that them list to draw them upoun hicht,
That it might be of nae manner of might,
To win that house by craft or subtlety,
Wherefore it is maist good alluterly;   entirely
Into my time wherever I have been,
Most fair, most goodly, most pleasant to be seen.

The town, the castle, and the pleasant land;
The sea wall is upon the other hand;
The Great Cross Kirk, and eik the Mason Dew;   *maison dieu*
The Jacobine friars of the white hue,
The Carmelites, and the monkis eik
Of the four orders were not to seek;
Thay were all into this town dwelling.

In line 13 the words *upoun hicht* refer to the Scottish medieval war tactic in which the lower parts were closed and the fighting was carried out from the upper works. The 'Great Cross Kirk' refers to a church with transepts giving it the form of a cross and probably refers to St Mary's near the modern Scotsgate. The Jacobine friars were the Dominicans, so called because their first settlement was in the church of St Jacques in Paris.

Medieval Berwick had three fully attested hospitals run by the clergy for the poor and the sick. The oldest, founded around 1234, was the hospital dedicated to St Edward the Confessor and cited by extant records as 'the hospital of the Bridge of Berwick', *Domus Pontis*. It was initially funded by the parish church of Kettins, Angus, and was administered by the Trinitarians. It is not known for sure when the hospital ceased to function, but it did not survive the fifteenth century. It is thought to have been sited at the end of the timber bridge destroyed in 1294 near to the modern boathouse of the Berwick Amateur Rowing Club (1869).

The hospice of *Maison Dieu*, initially at least a secular hospital, was founded around 1286 by Philip de Rydale, a local burgess, and supported in part by its rents on the lands at Bowsden. It was run by a master and 'poor brethren and sisters' and may have merged with the Trinitarians' hospital. The records are unclear and both *Domus Pontis* and *Maison Dieu* are sometimes referred to in the records by the latter name. A petition of 1333 says that *Maison Dieu* was destroyed by siege. It stood at the corner of Quay Walls and Bridge End. Up to 1835 Bridge End was known as 'Maison Dieu', as was the quay below it after 1336.

The hospital dedicated to St Mary Magdalene was founded before 1296 and lasted for about a hundred years. It suffered war damage and was restored by Edward II; it is likely that it was sited in the area of present-day Magdalene Fields lying to the north of Lords Mount.

Two more hospitals are mentioned; the least known house was that dedicated to the Frankish St Leonard and is thought to have been founded in 1297. Only one reference to the hospital has been found, a petition of Edward I for the restitution of lands in Liddesdale. Then there was the hospital at Berwick dedicated to St Mary the Virgin. This was founded in 1297 with a charter of 1330 or so and it was an almshouse for resident poor people and was run by one of the innumerable hospital orders following the rule of St Augustine of Hippo with a secular master. The actual site of the hospital is obscure and may have been outside the town walls; certainly, though, the brethren owned buildings and land in the town. The *Calendar of Inquisitions Post Mortem* records that in 1367 the master and brethren of the hospital had 'four acres adjoining the hospital belonging to its enclosure and within the churchyard of [*Berwick*]'.

There were five medieval churches in Berwick, and from the twelfth to the fourteenth centuries the town and environs were divided into two parishes. The first included the town and seaward lands and formed the area governed by Trinity church; the second area was Bondington and the westward territory.

Set within the village of Bondington (see page 6), the church of St Lawrence was deemed founded by Roger Fitzwilliam around 1128-58 for the monks of Kelso. The church was given to the monks of Durham in 1174. There is no mention of the church after 1300 and the historian J.Scott notes that a church 90ft long with a 25ft square tower at the west end was discovered with several graves during the building of Cheviot House, Castle Terrace, in the nineteenth century. The church is likely to have been of the Norman aisleless variety with simple nave and square chancel.

Medieval Holy Trinity church was described in 1648 as being 'very little' and 'meanly built' and was demolished during 1648-52 when the new church was built (see page 101). The medieval church appears in some chronicles as a foundation first belonging to Kelso Abbey, but was in the sway of Durham by 1156. At first it had a monastic rector and after 1360 a perpetual vicar. Named altars dedicated to St Mary the Blessed Virgin and St John the Divine are mentioned. It is noted too that on 15 April 1242, David de Bernham, Bishop of St Andrews, was in Berwick to perform the *reconciliato* (reconsecration) of Holy Trinity church after it had been polluted by the shedding of blood within its walls as a result of a quarrel between two *clerici scholares* (ordained clerks). The *Pontificale Ecclesiae Sancti Andreae* further records a chapel by the medieval bridge *pro Ministro et Fratribus Sanctae Trinitatis Pontis Berwici* (for the Minister and Brethren of the Holy Trinity of the Bridge of Berwick).

The church of the Blessed Mary, said to have been associated with the hospital (see page 37), was set by the Scotsgate near the junction with Walkergate. Its foundation in 1130 is mentioned in the *Coldingham Charters* and it was demolished around 1562 when a rampart was built. The church of St Nicholas stood near St Nicholas Tower on the medieval walls from 1281 (its policies at Kings Mount took in the cricket ground). An altar to St Eleme is mentioned as being founded by Edward III.

Both the historians J.Scott and W.Hutchinson mention a large church built in 1301 by Anthony Bec, Bishop of Durham (1284-1311), who acted as Edward I's envoy to the Scots at the time of the Treaty of Birgham (1290). Nothing further is known of the church or its location.

CHAPTER 4

The Developing Burgh

Berwick was to be directly involved in the Scottish struggle for independence, and under the three English kings called Edward, during the period 1272 to 1377, the town waxed and waned, suffered mightily, and was the scene of great affairs. On Alexander III's death in 1286, his heir was his three-year-old granddaughter Margaret, 'The Maid of Norway', and the Community of the Kingdom of Scotland (that is, the prelates and magnates in council assembled at Alexander's funeral at Dunfermline Abbey on 20 March 1286) appointed six Guardians of the Realm: the bishops of St Andrews and Glasgow, the earls of Fife and Buchan, John Comyn of Badenoch and James the Steward. Despite the oaths of allegiance to the new infant monarch, the succession to the Scottish throne was still regarded as uncertain. In due time little Margaret's father Eric of Norway, with the Scots and English, met at Salisbury to agree her future. The negotiations culminated in the Treaty of Birgham (1290) in which it was laid down that Margaret should marry Edward of Caernarvon, who in due time became Edward II. Margaret set out for Scotland but she died on the journey in late September 1290. Consequently the throne of Scotland was now irrefutably vacant and Berwick was to be involved in the momentous events to follow.

Anything might happen. Thirteen persons put forward claims to the throne and bloodshed seemed inevitable. From the castle of Leuchars, Fife, on the morrow of St Faith the Virgin, William Frazer, Bishop of St Andrews, wrote to Edward I, 'most excellent Prince...by the Grace of God, king of England, lord of Ireland, and Duke of Aquitaine'. The bishop commented on the jockeyings of the Scottish magnates. In effect the bishop, who recognised Edward's claim of feudal superiority over Scotland, was asking the king to act as umpire in the ensuing

The Great Seal of John Balliol (c.1250-1313), called 'Toom Tabard' (empty surcoat) by his contemporaries because of his ineffectuality and his inglorious reign. He was chosen King of Scots by Edward I in the Great Hall of Berwick Castle on 17 Nov. 1292. The Great Hall now lies under the platforms of Berwick's railway station.

debate on who should reign, although there was a heavy hint in his letter that one John Balliol would make a good king 'willing to abide by your council' (*dum tamen ille vestro consilio voluerit adhere*). Edward was not slow to take the hint.

It was soon clear that there were only three serious candidates for the throne: John Balliol, great-great-great grandson of David I; the octogenarian Robert Bruce, Earl of Annandale; and John Hastings, lord of Abergavenny, the grandson of Earl David's third daughter Ada, wife of Henry Hastings. Edward I was quite determined that any decision should be seen to come as a judgement of a court, with his own indisputable authority recognised to act as judge, and founded on legal tradition and examination of the historical bases of the claims. It was to be so.

The first phase of the 'great case' was enacted at the parish church of Norham on 10 May 1291. Various further assemblies were held to hear the case for Edward as 'judge' at Upsettlington and Norham Castle, and the outcome was that Edward was recognised by the claimants as *rex et superior dominus*

Scotiae (king and liege lord of the Scots), and Scotland was handed over into Edward's hands until a judgement be made.

The assessment now shifted to Berwick where hearings were conducted before Edward, twenty-four members of his council, and eighty assessors (forty appointed by Bruce, and forty by Balliol). The hearings began on 3 August 1291; Edward departed on a tour of Scotland on 5 August, and, as the king had so much work to do, the petitions of the main claimants were sealed in a sack and deposited in Berwick Castle until 2 June 1292 when the hearings were to be resumed. In total the hearings at Berwick lasted until 17 November 1292, when the justiciary Roger Brabazon, in the Great Hall of Berwick Castle, stepped forward and spoke in the king's name declaring judgement in favour of John Balliol.

Balliol made an unequivocal act of homage to Edward at Norham, and was installed at Scone on 30 November, and oaths of fealty were sworn at Newcastle on 26 December 1292. Berwick Castle (with twenty-two others) was handed over to John Balliol by the keeper Peter Burdett, and eighty-four Berwick burgesses swore fealty to Edward I. The king had spent most of the summer and winter of 1292 at Berwick, now by far the largest town in Scotland. While the political and diplomatic machinations continued, the burgesses of Berwick went about their affairs and those such as wine merchant Geoffrey of Berwick filled their coffers, for he had just done a deal with the prior of St Andrews to supply £20 worth of fine wine.

Edward I regarded the accession of the 42-year-old Anglo-Norman John Balliol as the beginning of a new phase of Anglo-Scottish relations with himself as dominant partner. An appeal to Edward by the burgess Master Roger Bartholomew of Berwick in 1292 underlines that, 'by divine providence', Edward was the real ruler of England, Scotland and Ireland and was being appealed to by Scottish officials and merchants alike for judgements in civil matters. Soon to be called 'Toom Tabard' (empty surcoat) by his fellow-countrymen, John Balliol was summoned into Edward's presence on the slightest pretext and he bent to the English monarch's will.

In 1294 Philip IV of France seized the English possessions of Gascony and Edward demanded that Balliol and the Scots render military service in France. Surrounded by his council of nobles who had gathered at Stirling in July 1295, Balliol, who had been willing to accede to Edward's demands, was forced by the nobles to decline to obey Edward. Englishmen were ejected from their Scottish estates and Scotland entered into negotiations with France. Edward was furious.

Along with Roxburgh and Jedburgh castles, Balliol was required to surrender Berwick Castle for the duration of the ensuing war, and Edward issued writs to seize Balliol's lands and goods, and those of all who supported him. The Scots, leaving Balliol behind, gathered on the Border and made encroachments into Northumberland and Cumberland. On 28 March the English army crossed the Tweed at Coldstream and Norham and by way of Hutton arrived at the outskirts of Berwick where they pitched camp on the south-east slopes of Halidon Hill; Edward set up his quarters at the nunnery of the Blessed Mary and St Leonard at Halystone. The English fleet, now set in Berwick roads, tried to attack the castle from the Tweed, but were repulsed and retired after some of their boats had been grounded in the mud. Meanwhile Edward, mounted on his favourite horse Bayard, moved his army across what is now the Meadows and Newfields and entered Berwick town. The burgh was taken with very little difficulty and the slaughter of the inhabitants began. Some 7000 people perished that day, with 'bloode enough to runne the mills'. The historian George Ridpath noted that the only real opposition to Edward's army came from 'thirty Flandrian merchants' who defended their 'strong tower, called the Red Hall'; these defenders were eventually overwhelmed too and put to the sword. Sir William Douglas surrendered Berwick Castle, and on 5 April 1296 Edward received John Balliol's formal *diffidatio*, or declaration of homage and fealty, in the royal chambers there.

Edward now paused to strengthen Berwick. Ditchers, masons, carpenters and smiths all converged on Berwick to replace the flimsy outworks with deep ditch and broad earthworks. A 'new town' was designed to act as Edward's financial capital with an Exchequer (see page 26); a new centre of trade was established, and those burgesses of Berwick who had thwarted him were displaced. By now Edward was fully convinced that he had totally defeated the Scots, particularly after their rout at Dunbar by John de Warenne, Earl of Surrey. The whole of Lothian had been overrun and Edinbugh Castle subdued.

M.A.Denham tells us in his *Tracts* that while Edward was assaulting Berwick certain 'rhymes' were made about him. They were quoted by Robert Fabyan (d.1513) in *The Concordance of Histories*:

> What weyns king Edward with his long shankes
> To have wonne Berwick, all our unthankes?
> Gaas pykes hym
> And when he hath it
> Gaas dykes him.

When the Scots were subsequently beaten at Dunbar, one cleric penned these contemporary rhymes quoted by Thomas Wright (1810-77), the antiquary, in his *Essays*:

> These scattered Scottes
> Hold we for sottes
> Of wrenches unware;
> Early in the morning
> In an evil timing
> Came they to Dunbar.

There followed a series of humiliations for Balliol and the Scots. The Scottish regalia, holy relics like Queen Margaret's Black Rood, and state records were seized, and a series of submissions were extracted from the magnates. John Balliol abdicated at Montrose and Edward took possession of the Stone of Destiny, which rested for a while at Berwick Castle on its journey to England to be set within the coronation chair of Westminster Abbey.

On 22 August, Edward returned to Berwick and there held parliament to order the affairs of his realm. John Balliol had surrendered his kingdom to Edward and was on his way to

The Great Seal, skull and coins of Robert I, the Bruce (1274-1329),
King of Scots. Victor over Edward II at Bannockburn in 1314, the
great patriotic King captured Berwick on 2 April 1318, and starved the
castle into submission some eleven weeks later. This loss of Berwick to
the Scots was a severe blow to the English. The castle was surrendered
to the English again in 1333 and in total was captured or sacked
fourteen times.

virtual house arrest in Hertford; when William Wallace rose in
Balliol's name in 1297, Balliol and his young son were
transferred to the Tower. Balliol was allowed to leave England
in 1299 and he died at his French castle of Hélicourt in
Normandy in 1313.

At Berwick, where he tarried a month or so, Edward received
the homage of prelate and magnate; indeed Berwick castle and
town were swelled to capacity at this time with people from
most of the Scottish shires. The *Documents Illustrative of the History
of Scotland* tells us how 'a strong body' of Gascons (from the
ancient province in south-west France) were lodged at Berwick
garrison, and they probably helped in the repair of the
fortifications, 1297-98. (There seems to have been a Gascon
presence in Berwick for some time as *Barbour's Bruce Book*
records that the Gascon Edmund de Cailow was in command of
Berwick in 1316.)

Edward now appointed John de Warenne guardian of the lands, Sir Hugh de Cressingham treasurer, and Sir Walter of Amersham chancellor. Then, as the chronicler Andrew, the apostolic notary, said, Edward set out for the south 'on the Sunday after the feast of the Holy Cross' (16 September 1296). But he retired south having made a grave mistake: he left the throne of Scotland vacant. His enemies were now just biding their time.

From 1296 to 1306 there was an interregnum in Scotland and the country was troubled and restive. At Berwick Castle the justiciar monitored the situation on the Borders and the barons, Henry Percy and Robert Clifford, were given the task of surveying the movements of the Scottish magnates. One in particular interested the English. Sir William Douglas, who had been the keeper of Berwick Castle, was the first Scottish baron to desert Edward. Douglas was taken prisoner and brought in chains to the castle he had once governed and was subsequently transferred to the Tower of London where he died. In 1297 Sir William Wallace, who had been born around 1270 the son of Sir Malcolm Wallace of Elderslie in Renfrewshire, killed an English sheriff at Lanark and supporters flocked to his side. As the Scottish army grew, stronghold after stronghold fell and the English forces of de Warenne and Cressingham were vanquished at Stirling Bridge on 11 September 1297. For a while, records the *Chronicle of Lanercost*, the Scots held Berwick town but were never able to take the castle. The Scottish victors at Stirling Bridge made a raid into Northumberland and Cumberland and Wallace assumed the title of the Guardian of Scotland in John Balliol's name. Wallace now informed the towns of the Low Countries that they could begin to trade once more with an independent Scotland, and for the moment the Scots paused for breath to await Edward's reaction. They did not have to wait long.

The Scots vacated Berwick town and Edward advanced across the Border to defeat Wallace's forces at Falkirk on 22 July 1298. Wallace 'The Liberator' now took to the forests, but in time he was betrayed and Sir John Menteith handed him over to

Edward. Wallace was tried at Westminster Hall and was found guilty and executed on 24 August 1305. Pieces of his dismembered body were displayed from London Bridge to Stirling as a warning, and his left arm was exhibited at Berwick. It is said that today's Wallace Green takes its name from the site where Wallace's arm was displayed: in fairness, others attribute the name to the description, 'the green by the walls'.

Through his 'Ordinance for the Government of Scotland', Edward I made a final attempt to solve his northern problems and Berwick was his administrative headquarters and arsenal. Out of the Scottish mists had come another hero, Robert Bruce, the son of Robert Bruce, Earl of Annandale and Carrick and the grandson of Robert Bruce, 'the claimant' to the Scottish throne. Young Bruce had once served on the English side (for the Bruces had never recognised Balliol's right to the throne), but had thrown in his lot with Wallace in 1297. His burning desire was to be king and he was egged on by such devious patriots as Berwick-born William de Lamberton, Bishop of St Andrews. It was a sudden violent deed that gave Bruce the impetus to act. On 10 February 1306, Bruce met John Comyn of Badenoch, Balliol's nephew and the regent, to confer alone in the church of the Greyfriars, Dumfries. They quarrelled and Bruce stabbed Comyn, who was despatched by Bruce's squires before the high altar. It was a sacrilegious act and Bruce was faced with two alternatives. Was he to flee Scotland? Or was he to seize the throne? He chose the latter, and on 27 March 1306 he was placed on the throne at Scone by Isabella, Countess of Buchan, representing her brother the Earl of Fife. This lady was to appear in Berwick's story a little later.

All this time Berwick was used as an administrative headquarters in the north and writs and documents were dated as from the castle. From time to time the burgesses witnessed displays of medieval pomp and circumstance. On Sunday, the Feast of St Hilary, 1304, Edward I's second wife, Queen Margaret of France, passed through Berwick on her way to Dirleton Castle.

Up to 1296 it can be said that Berwick was a religious and

commercial centre, whereas after that date it became a depot
for supplies for activities in southern Scotland and northern
England. By 1302 weekly markets had been introduced and the
street system was being developed. For instance *Burghgate* (part
of modern Castlegate), *Huddinggate*, *Uddyngate* and *Soutergate*
(the first two making up Church Street, the third a part of
Castlegate, but after 1333 it referred to Church Street) were
being evolved, as was *Crossgate* (Woolmarket), *Fleshwergate*,
Fishergate (near the waterfront), *Fowtheriengang* (St Aidan's
church passage), *Hidegate* (Silver Street), Hide Hill, *Kings Gerner*
(by the south-east side of Cowgate), *Quarrelgate*, *Scyren Lane*,
Seagate Street, *Sissergate* (in Castlegate), The Snook, Walkergate,
Wallace Green and *Watergate* (Sandgate). All these would be in
place as burgess dwelling areas by 1336.

The Berwick burgess of the Middle Ages was a family man,
with wife and children and maybe a widowed mother and an
unmarried sister or two in his household. He was at the top of
the burgh heap with the *stallagers* a rung or two beneath him.
The *stallagers* were the market stallholders who enjoyed fewer
burgh privileges and paid fewer dues on property and trade.
Some of the traders formed themselves into partnerships called
societates. Below them still were the craftsmen, the journeymen,
the labourers and the servants, with their own families. At the
bottom of the heap were the poor, the chronically sick and
disabled, the lepers and the beggars who were aided one way or
another by the religious orders.

A typical Berwick burgess's house of the Middle Ages was like
the one found during the demolition of 9 Marygate in 1962.
The first ten feet of the wall was usually sandstone and
whinstone, with another ten feet of 'claut and clay', the clay
reinforced with barley straw. The rafter wood was usually axe-
hewn oak. Up to the fifteenth century roofs would normally be
thatched; the first non-imported pantiles were made at Lowick
around 1480. Servants occupied the rear of the building.

The Berwick burgesses were free men and they held land
within the burgh and their rank passed down from father to
son. Some burgesses held land outwith the burgh; for instance

in 1307 William Stobbe was granted a *lovate* (an oxgang—13 acres) of land by William Ridel at the Flemings' hamlet of Flemington. The burgesses had the privileges of trading within the king's burgh, and they had the right of first choice to buy from incoming|boats: indeed, even if a boat was driven into Berwick harbour by storms, the master was duty bound to display his cargo for the burgesses to buy whether he had intended to call at Berwick or not. The king's chamberlain paid regular visits to oversee the burgh's financial affairs, and spoke to the chief officer about the running of the burgh. In time the chief officer was an alderman (*praepositus*) elected by the burgesses, and in the case of Berwick he was given the title of mayor. Some time after 1235 by order of Alexander II Berwick was the only Scottish town to have a mayor. The office of *praepositus* developed into a council of twenty-four by 1249, which was the year in which the guild regulations, *Statutae Gildae*, were drawn up (see page 20). The monastic documents of the day record the wealth of several of Berwick's fourteenth-century burgesses. One such was John of Chilton, who was mayor of Berwick in 1336; at one time his wool exports accounted for some fifteen percent of Berwick's total exports and he was an important agent for Coldingham priory. John of Chilton and others usually fled when the town changed hands and he seems to have thrown in his lot with Edward I.

By the early 1300s Robert Bruce now had to face up to a bitter reality. One of the foremost towns in Scotland, Berwick, was firmly in the hands of the English; his country was occupied; and he was anathema in Christendom, having been excommunicated for Comyn's murder on holy ground. In Scotland too he had many enemies. In June 1306 Edward I's commander in Scotland, Aymer de Valence, Earl of Pembroke, defeated Bruce at Methven, and he fled to the hills—where legend has it that he was hounded by dogs and encouraged by spiders. Twelve of Bruce's knights, captured at Methven, were hanged at Berwick, one of them his beloved brother Nigel. Within a period of less than a year his womenfolk were prisoners, three of his brothers had been executed, and the

Countess of Buchan, who had assisted in his coronation, was a prisoner herself.

It has long been a tradition that Isabella, Countess of Buchan, was imprisoned in a wooden cage and hung from the walls of Berwick Castle. The misconception comes from the French word *cage*, a prison of iron and timber placed within a turret. There is no evidence at all that she was hung from the wall; instead she would be viewed through the *cage's* lattice wall. There she remained until 1310 when she was released from her ordeal into the protection of the Carmelite friary at Berwick, and in 1313 she was placed in the custody of her nephew-in-law, Sir Henry Beaumont. Bruce's daughter Marjorie was also kept in a similar *cage* in the Tower of London.

By early 1307 Bruce staged a comeback in the west. He defeated his enemies at Glen Trool, and avenged his rout at Methven by defeating the Earl of Pembroke at Loudon Hill. Just as he was about to face the full might of his adversaries, he heard that Edward I had died at Burgh-on-Sands on 7 July 1307.

The new king, Edward II, gave up the Scottish campaign and turned to more frivolous pursuits, although in due time he ordered twenty ships to strengthen coastal defences, particularly his castle at Berwick, against attack by sea and Scottish incursions down the coast. In 1309 the English army gathered at Berwick and raided Scotland. The campaign was a failure and Edward and his Queen, Isabella of France, wintered at Berwick, but Edward enjoyed more the arms of his lover Piers Gaveston, Earl of Cornwall, than he did Isabella's. *The Household Book of Queen Isaballa of England* (1311-12), written by William de Boudon, Keeper of the Wardrobe, offers a fascinating account of the costs of the queen's stay at Berwick. So much paraphernalia went with the queen that a large portion of her possessions had to come to Berwick by boat watched over by the queen's ewerer (*aquario*), John de Drayton, who supervised four cartloads (*plaustris*) of clothes and a cartload of spices.

With Berwick as a storehouse, booming with the increased trade in war supplies, another campaign against the Scots was launched in 1310. It too made little headway. Another was launched in 1311, but all the while, although Bruce possessed no siege engines, he was successful in surprise night attacks on the castles and camps of the English which won him Linlithgow, Perth, Dundee, Edinburgh and Roxburgh; but a surprise attack on Berwick failed. The *Chronicle of Lanercost* tells us that the castle and town were saved during this raid by the barking of a dog which alerted the lookouts.

By 1313 only Stirling remained in English hands. There Edmund Bruce parleyed with the English commander, Sir Philip de Mowbray, and conjointly they agreed that if an English army had not come to relieve it by midsummer 1314, then the castle of Stirling would surrender. Edward II sent out writs to his magnates that they should meet him with their men-at-arms at Berwick on 10 June 1314. Edward and his 20,000-strong army left Berwick on 17 June and met Bruce with his 7000 troops at Bannockburn. The rest is history; Edward II was defeated and returned to Berwick by boat from Dunbar to which he had fled. In September 1314 he left Berwick for his parliament at York.

From the chronicles of the Wiltshire abbey of Malmesbury we have this note on Berwick in 1315: 'A strong and well-walled town...it has nothing to fear on the part of the sea'. Strong it was, for it repulsed Bruce's attempts to take it during the 'octaves of Epiphany' of 15 January 1316. During 1316-18 Berwick was defended by Gascons, who also made raids into Scotland. Indeed Berwick retained its cosmopolitan flavour for, like the Flemings, merchants from Cologne had established their 'factory'—the 'White Halla'—in Seagait.

At last, in 1319, Bruce took Berwick and entrusted its defences to Walter, High Steward of Scotland; the town, said Barbour, had been betrayed to him by a burgess, Peter Spalding, an enemy of the governor, for money and land. The loss of Berwick was a symbolic blow to Edward II and it had to be retaken. An army of 8000 besieged the town and castle from their camp outside the walls, which witnesses tell us was 'as big as any town'. Even though he had the support of the fleet which blockaded Berwick roads, Edward was repulsed. During the siege the English used a 'great machine' (called a *sow*, a movable shed for protecting besiegers), and the destruction of the sow led to a local saying to describe a scheme that has gone astray: 'The sow has farrowed'.

Bruce was now complete master of Berwick castle and town, where he dated charters and assembled a parliament.

His position for the moment secure, he now set about strengthening Berwick's defences which had been restructured by Edward I. When Edward captured Berwick on Good Friday 1296, he would find no fortifications really worthy of the name, except for the castle. His first task was the construction of a *stank* (ditch), 80ft by 40ft, from the outworks of the castle to the River Tweed; in this way he encircled the town to the north and east by the earthwork known as the Edwardian Fosse. Before the end of Edward II's reign, 1307-27, a wall varying from fifteen to twenty-two feet high (with nineteen interlinking towers) was constructed along the inner edge of the Fosse, and extended to completely surround the town, a circuit of two and a half miles. It was this wall that was materially improved by Robert Bruce during 1318-33. The remains of these walls are referred to as 'The Edwardian Walls' and remain *in situ* only to an extent of some sixty yards.

From the castle the Edwardian Walls were set out to the east (running parallel with modern Northumberland Avenue). The Edwardian Fosse is now covered by the Castle garage, the Bell Tower school (1903) and the gardens of villas of Belltower Park at this point; within the area of the garage to the end of the villas stood Broad Stair Head Tower and a Defensive Tower. From the end of the villas the Edwardian Walls emerge, and within the middle of the earthen mound stands the Bell Tower. This four-storey, octagonal tower of around 1576-77 has been considerably altered at various dates and is set on an Edwardian base. The wall to each side of the tower has been demolished to its lowest courses, but the doorways which give access to the parapet walk show the original height of the 9ft-thick wall which replaced Edward I's wooden palisade.

Isabel of Fife, Countess of Buchan, wife of John Comyn and sister of Earl Duncan IV, was imprisoned in a *cage* in Berwick Castle in 1306 for her part in Robert I's coronation. She it was who, as a member of the Clan Macduff, had led King Robert to his enthronement at his coronation at Scone on Palm Sunday, 27 March 1306. Isabel was incarcerated for her pains at Berwick until June 1310 whereupon she was removed to the house of the Carmelites in the town. This stylised watercolour of her is by the Dundee artist Stewart Carmichael (1867-1950) and was painted in 1908 (*Museum & Art Galleries, Dundee*).

Past the Bell Tower the wall links with Lord's Mount at the north-east angle of the medieval walls. This circular fortification was set out in the reign of Henry VIII in 1539, was fit for use in 1535 and was completed in 1542; the tower was excavated during 1972-73 to reveal an oven, fireplaces, a well and a privy. Sitting below Lord's Mount is Magdalene Field House, and behind can be seen the ditch known as Spades Mire. From the site of the Tapee Loch the first section of Spades Mire traverses the railway cutting and runs along the back of the former grammar school, across the land known as Coneygarth to the road by the holiday camp. The second section runs across the camp site to Magdalene Fields to the cliff above the old bathing pool. The date of construction of Spades Mire and actual function are unknown, but it is undoubtedly medieval and may well have linked the Tapee Loch with a water defence system.

From Lord's Mount the Edwardian Wall runs south-east in fragments in which were placed Wallace Gate with the 'Murderer Tower', Middle Tower and Red Tower, to the site of the *batardeau*, the water-dam for the later Elizabethan moat; the water for this also came from the Tapee Loch. Cutting across the modern golf course is a traverse, known as the Covered Way; this linked the Elizabethan Wall with a garrison and battery by the edge of the cliff; the old road to Edinburgh ran along the south-east of this traverse. The Edwardian Wall runs under the Brass Bastion at this point.

The Edwardian Wall proceeds south, and between Lord's Mount and the south of the river were eight flanking towers running across The Stanks recreation ground and past the Elizabethan Cowport Gate to 'the Great Bulwark of the Snook'. 'Snook' means a projecting piece of land, and hereabouts can be seen medieval rigs and furrows which were cultivated well into the sixteenth century. Here can be traced the unfinished Edwardian gateway which led into the area by Holy Trinity Church, now called Wallace Green. The wall then ran down the cliff above Pier Road at Flagstaff Park and terminated at the now-vanished St Nicholas Tower near the west end of modern Devon Terrace. The name of the tower is undoubtedly taken from the chapel (see page 39) somewhere in the vicinity dedicated to the fourth-century St Nicholas, Bishop of Myra.

From King's Mount the Elizabethan and Edwardian Walls coincide, but between Longstone View Terrace and Ness Gate is the Black Watchtower, the only remaining Edwardian Tower. The Edwardian Walls now run under the Elizabethan Walls to emerge at the end of Love Lane below Meg's Mount. The Edwardian Walls then follow the riverside to rise above the modern Castle Vale Park to cross the railway forecourt and Castlegate. From the site of today's Castle Hotel, the Edwardian Wall linked by a spur with St Mary Gate and the castle's northeasterly tower.

For the next few years after Berwick's capture by Bruce, the burgh saw peace and the people went about their business. Indeed a thirteen-year peace was signed at Bishopthorpe, near York, on 30 May 1323 and was ratified at Berwick by Bruce on 7 June in royal council. To secure his position, though, Bruce set about frequent raids to harry the English. For a time Edward I had been called *Malleus Scottorum* (Hammer of the Scots); the counter soubriquet, *Malleus Anglorum*, appealed to Bruce. But Bruce's heir, Edward, king of Ireland since 1317, died in 1318 and a succession problem arose.

It was decided that should Bruce die without surviving children, the crown would pass to his grandson Robert, son of Bruce's daughter Marjorie and Walter the High Steward, 'defender of Berwick'. In 1324, however, a son was born to Bruce and his second wife Elizabeth de Burgh and a new arrangement had to be made. Berwick was represented at the parliament which met at Cambuskenneth in 1326 to swear allegiance to the new heir.

All was not well in England. Edward II's queen Isabella, who since a bride had endured Edward's homosexual preferences yet dutifully had borne him four children, now openly supported his enemies while she was on a diplomatic mission to her brother, the King of France. One of these enemies, Roger Mortimer, became her lover, and together they plotted an invasion of England on behalf of her elder son Edward. They invaded England in 1326 and Edward II was captured and deposed. His son was crowned as Edward III and in September 1327 Edward II was put to death in the dungeon of Berkeley Castle by the hideous means of a red-hot poker thrust into his anus.

Meanwhile the Scots were keeping up the pressure on the Border and on 4 April 1327 a Scottish siege of Berwick began. By 16th May Edward III had arrived at Tweedmouth (Parliament Street traditionally marks the site of his encampment), but the English ships were repulsed at the mouth of the Tweed. The town was unsuccessfully blockaded and the English retired.

By 1327 an important agreement affecting Scotland was reached through the Treaty of Northampton. England renounced claim to the homage of Scotland; England recognised Scotland's right to sovereignty; Bruce was to compensate Edward III to the tune of £20,000 for giving up his rights in Scotland; an indenture of marriage was agreed between Edward's sister Joanna and David Bruce the king's son; and as a part of the marriage contract the Coronation Stone which had been removed by Edward I was to be returned. On 15 July 1328, escorted by the Bishop of Lincoln, Chancellor of England, Edward III's queen, Philippa of Hainault, travelled to Berwick with the princess Joanna. There they were met by Robert Randolph, Earl of Moray, and Lord James Douglas. The entry into Berwick was a sumptuous affair and the quays hummed with the unloading of food and products of the Low Countries for the wedding feast. The young princess was six and the prince five. From such documents as the *Calendar of Close Rolls* we see that the good folk of Berwick enjoyed piles of beef, mutton, *bacones* (salt pork), and oats, peas and beans in profusion with generous helpings of fish soup, herrings and dried fish from Gascony. There was to be one sour note: the abbot of Westminster refused to allow the return of the Coronation Stone.

Robert Bruce died at Cardross on 11 May 1329, and once more Berwick was in the forefront of events.

CHAPTER 5

The Siege of Berwick and the
Battle of Halidon Hill

David II was six years old when his reign began, and he was anointed and crowned at Scone, on 24 November 1331, in the atmosphere of independence and sovereignty that his father had won. However, the essential element of leadership was lacking and ultimately David II lost all that his father had gained. At first, Sir Thomas Randolph, Earl of Moray, was appointed Guardian of the Realm, but he died in 1332. Edward Balliol, the erstwhile King John's son, now landed at Kinghorn in August 1332 with a group of disgruntled nobles disinherited by Robert Bruce, and he defeated the new Guardian, Sir Archibald Douglas, Earl of Mar. Balliol had himself crowned at Scone on 24 September 1332. Although he had to beat a hasty retreat in his shirt tails and on an unsaddled horse after a skirmish at Annan, Balliol was back in 1333 with Edward III to besiege Berwick. Edward had been assisting Balliol secretly since the latter's return and Balliol had agreed that the town, castle and county of Berwick would be Edward's part-payment for assistance.

The siege of Berwick proper began on 12 April 1333 under the command of Lord William Montague. Edward had arrived at Tweedmouth on 9 May and the necessary provisions and arms were in place and the English fleet was in position. Within the town Sir William Keith led the resistance, Sir Alexander Seton was warden, and the castle was defended by Patrick of Dunbar, Earl of March. In the siege of 1319, a key man in the skilful defence had been 'the versatile Fleming' John Crabb; now he was helping the attackers (Crabb had been taken prisoner at Roxburgh Bridge a short while before). Crabb knew Berwick's weaknesses, the positions of sentries and the numbers of arms. Two of the engines of war in the attack had been specially made by Richard the Goldsmith at Cowick in

Yorkshire; one siege engine came from York Castle. These engines were transported to Berwick from Hull, Sir William de la Pole tells us, aboard the *Gracedieu*, the *Jonete* and the *Nicholas*, with 691 rounds of stone missiles. Some small firearms were used, but Berwick was to enter military history as the first British town to be bombarded by cannon. The English chronicle, *The Brut*, tells us the besiegers 'made meny assaultes with gonnes and with othere engynes to the toune, wherwith thai destroiede meny a fair house; an cherches also were beten adoune vnto the erthe, with gret stones, and spitouse camyng out of gonnes and of othere gynnes'.

Edward III soon realised that the town and castle could not be taken easily, so he retired into the Scottish hinterland, and after taking Edinburgh Castle he harried the country as far as Scone and Dundee. Then he made his way back to Berwick and found that it was still holding out against the troops he had left behind. By this time the Maison Dieu was 'utterly cast down' and the great hall of the castle and a tower were badly damaged. The *Rotuli Parliamentorum* says that Berwick itself was 'greatly destroyed'.

Edward now crossed the Tweed and set up his camp on the south side of the river, from where he blockaded the town by land and sea. The chronicles of Walsingham Abbey record a piece of bad luck for the town's defenders. Part of the English fleet was detached and sailed up the Tweed to the town walls where lookouts gave the alarm. Tar-soaked faggots were prepared to fire the ships, but the flames from the burning faggots set the town alight. The English gloated at the 'divine judgement' that destroyed a large part of Berwick.

A truce was sought, but next morning the defenders of Berwick changed their minds and Edward's attack continued. Then the tired combatants within the walls negotiated a fifteen-day truce and surrendered twelve hostages with the agreement that if they had not been relieved by 11 July they would totally capitulate to Edward. As the hostages were handed over, messengers galloped off to inform the Scottish Guardian of their plight. On receipt of the message Sir Archibald Douglas

The concrete blocks on the south side of the River Tweed recall the siege of 'Fortress Britain' during 1939-45, while across the river the castle's Water Tower and White Wall recall the days when Berwick was besieged by both the English and the Scots. To the left the braes of Tommy the Miller's fields — a good place to view the west elevation of the castle — rise up to modern Castle Terrace (*Neil Potts*).

set on the march the great host of men at arms that he had been collecting, and on 11 July the Scottish force crossed the Tweed at Yair Ford, 'the ford by the fish trap'. Four great divisions of the Scots army descended upon unsuspecting Tweedmouth; across the river Edward and his army watched impotently while the Scots laid fire to it.

From Tweedmouth shore, at low tide, the Scots threw victuals and arms to the besieged town; and, crossing the precarious fabric of the old bridge, Sir William Keith, Sir Alexander Grey and Sir William Prenderguest led two hundred horsemen into Briggate past the smouldering ruin of the Maison Dieu. Before this entry was completed, however, Sir William Montague circled the seaward side of the town and cut off further deployment and incursion.

On 12 July 1333 the Scottish army were drawn up at

Sunnyside, on the hill just south of medieval Tweedmouth. It was an exercise designed to flaunt the might of the army, and messengers were sent to warn Edward that if he did not immediately call off the siege of Berwick, the Scots would systematically lay waste to England. Edward refused to be intimidated and the Scots army moved southwards leaving a trail of destruction. To give him extra bargaining power the Scots commander, Sir Archibald Douglas, laid siege to Bamburgh Castle, where Edward's queen, Philippa, had been residing since 27 May. Edward made no move to rescue her as he believed that Berwick would fall before Bamburgh.

Meanwhile messengers were sent to Edward from Berwick asking for the return of the hostages. The townsfolk believed that as Sir Archibald Douglas had arrived, this constituted a rescue according to the terms agreed. Edward argued the point and countered that if the town did not yield, the hostages would be forfeited. The townsfolk remained adamant that they had effectively been rescued and refused to surrender. Edward prepared for retribution.

A high gallows was set up for the execution of the most prominent hostage, Thomas Seton, son of Sir Alexander Seton, and he was hanged before his father's eyes on the north bank of the Tweed within close sight of the castle. This was the Setons' third son to die—Alexander was killed the day Balliol had landed at Kinghorn on 6 August 1332, and William Seton had been drowned while fighting amongst the English ships in the Tweed—and the chronicler Prior Andrew of Wyntoun, in his *Orygynale Cronikil of Scotland*, tells us that Lady Seton backed her husband in his resolve: she 'prayed hyre Lord, that he suld nought for that sycht sary be, and set not lytill be that skathe, for in honoure thai deyde aff thaiselff and all thare kyn'.

Edward now ordered that a number of the hostages should be executed each day in sight of the town until they were all dead. To save lives the defenders of Berwick agreed with Edward to surrender the castle on 20 July 1333 if they were not rescued by Sir Archibald Douglas. A truce was called and new terms were discussed as to how such a rescue should be defined.

The 'rescue' had to fulfil one of three stipulations: it would be effected if the Scots army successfully forced its way across the Tweed at the fishery called Berwick Stream or if (by Vespers on 19 July) the Scots army won a battle within the peninsula on which Berwick stood or if a division of two hundred men forced their way through the English lines with a loss of no more than thirty men. Edward also agreed that if the surrender took place, those townsfolk who wished to leave Berwick could do so with their goods and chattels without let or hindrance.

All this was communicated to Sir Archibald Douglas who was still harrying the lands around Morpeth. Sir Archibald knew that he had little alternative now but to return to Berwick. A pitched battle seemed inevitable, and Edward deployed his men with care. His army was assembled outside Berwick in the area of modern Castle Terrace and the Meadows. He placed two hundred men on the north bank of the Tweed to monitor the movements of the Scots army as it moved along the southlands of the Tweed and located five hundred men to keep watch on the defenders of the castle and town, lest they attempt any action to his rear in the event of a battle. Edward then positioned the rest of his troops on the top of Halidon Hill. Meanwhile, Prior Wyntoun tells us, the Scots army crossed the Tweed and camped at Duns to the far west of Edward's position at a distance of around fifteen miles. There Sir Archibald Douglas mulled over what he should do and came to the resolve that he had no option but to engage in battle.

Just after dawn on 19 July 1333 the Scottish army set off from Duns to Berwick to avert the surrender of the town by the following sunrise. From Halidon Hill the English had a panoramic view of the Tweed valley right up to Duns, but to the north there is a range of slopes about Edington Hill and Fouldon Hill which blocks the view. The Scottish army took this road (the B655 from Chirnside to Ayton) and emerged by Witches Knowe, then known as Bothulle.

By this time the English scouts had reported the movements of the Scots, and by midday Edward placed his army in the three divisions of the usual battle plan in a curve to suit the slopes of

Halidon Hill. To the right, nearest the sea, was Sir Edward Bohun, the Earl Marshal, representing his brother the Earl of Hereford, as constable. In the centre was Edward himself, and on his left was Edward Balliol's division; all three divisions had their subsidiary wings made up mostly of archers who supplied an effective angle of crossfire. Sir Radulph Basset and Sir Thomas Fourneville protected the army's rear.

Edward decided that his best tactic was to be defensive and he directed his men-at-arms to fight on foot. All the main action was to take place to the north of the present A6105. When the scouts reported the approach of the Scots, the English horse were despatched to the rear, and after he had addressed his army from horseback, Edward dismounted and stood at the head of his division.

As the Scots army advanced across Deans Hill they saw the English scouts at Mordington, and the commanders were now able to assess one another's strength. The Scottish army now crossed Mordington Bridge and advanced towards the present New West Farm. As they advanced, they blundered into the marshes. Sir Archibald Douglas ordered his men-at-arms to form into four 'battles' and cross this treacherous ground (now long drained) at the pace of the footsoldiers. The Scots' horse were left concealed in the plantations at Witches Knowe, and by now the Scots divisions were clear to the English. The first was commanded by John, Earl of Moray, the next by Robert, the High Steward, the third by the Earls of Ross, Sutherland and Strathearn, and the fourth by Sir Archibald Douglas himself. In all they totalled about 60,000.

As had happened at Bannockburn, a single combat preceded the battle in full sight of both armies. The chronicler Geoffrey le Baker describes the Scottish champion, one Raoul Turnbull, as a 'Goliath'. Turnbull, with his great mastiff alongside him, taunted the English to fight, and his challenge was taken up by Sir Robert Benhale of Edward's household. Turnbull and his dog were swiftly despatched. As he waited for the Scots to make a move, Edward must have been happy with his position. He held the initiative and his army was positioned at the top of a slope. The Scots had to descend from their position over a treacherous bog, and as they struggled through the mud the English bowmen were to take a savage toll: five hundred Scots troops alone fell at Heavyside slope.

While Moray and Stewart clashed with Balliol and Edward, Sir Archibald Douglas confronted Sir Edward Bohun; Sir Archibald had with him the men-at-arms he had chosen to break through after his lunge and relieve Berwick. It was the Earl of Moray's division which broke first before Balliol's troops and the steady rain of arrows, and the other two divisions lost heart. Soon all of the Scottish divisions were a disorderly mass. There were pockets of individual bravery, like that of Hugh, Earl of Ross, who with his men fought to the death. By this time the English chargers were brought up and Edward headed his cavalry to route the Scots (the Scots grooms at Witches Knowe saved their own skins and took the Scottish horses with them).

Few Scots magnates escaped the carnage and the bodies of the Scots lay strewn over a wide range between Halidon Hill and the Tweed; there was little quarter given and many Scots soldiers drowned in the sea trying to escape. As dusk fell, Edward called back his army, and while his men searched for booty amongst the corpses, he made a tally of the Scots noblemen who lay dead. Sir Archibald Douglas had been slain, and John Campbell, the Earl of Atholl, Alexander Bruce, Earl of Carrick, Malcolm, Earl of Lennox and Kenneth, Earl of Sutherland were all dead. The outcome had been inevitable: how could the Scots have won, said the *Chronicle of Lanercost*, when even a 'a vision of the crucified Christ, brandishing a spear' had come against the Scots from the direction of Berwick?

A memorial to the battle was set up (at noon on the battle's 600th anniversary) on 19 July 1933 by the Berwick Naturalists' Club. The stone, taken from Doddington quarry, was unveiled by the club's president, Major G.J. Logan-Home of Edrom, and is still in place at the edge of the A6105, Berwick-Duns road, just before Brow-of-the-Hill farm. Just east of Camphill farm, and reached along the minor road off the A6105, is a tourist viewpoint which is a good place to survey the battlefield and the boundaries of Berwick. It was constructed by the Rotary Club of Berwick-upon-Tweed to celebrate their golden jubilee in 1979; new descriptive panels were set up there in 1985 by Northumberland County Council.

The story of the Battle of Halidon Hill had been told to Sir Walter Scott by Mrs Margaret Swinton (sister of his maternal grandmother), and his subsequent *Halidon Hill: A dramatic sketch from Scottish history* was written at the request of Joanna Baillie and published on 25 June 1822. The publisher Robert Cadell gave Sir Walter £1000 for the script, and according to Scott's son-in-law and biographer J.G.Lockhart, it was written on 'two rainy mornings'. Scott designed it 'to illustrate military antiquities, and the manners of chivalry'.

On the feast day of St Margaret of Antioch (20 July), Edward III gave thanks for his victory at Halidon with a mass at the high altar of the convent of Halyston and endowed an altar in the chapel of this Cistercian nunnery in honour of the saint. He also paid for the war damage done to the convent during the skirmishes with the Scots; tradition has it that the nuns had attended to the wounded on both sides during the conflict. One hundred captives were now executed as an example, and the dead on both sides were buried in hallowed ground, which must have meant within the policies of the nunnery.

Edward now turned his thoughts to Berwick, whose capitulation was total. By 25 July 1333 he had appointed three administrators. Lord Henry de Percy became Warden of both town and castle and overseer of Border defences. Thomas de Bamburgh became Chancellor, and the office of Chamberlain, Sheriff, Keeper of Victuals and Fortifications was invested in Robert of Tong Hall. Scots clerics were displaced by English, those within Berwick's environs who had co-operated with Edward III were rewarded and the palms of helpful burgesses at Berwick were greased. English merchants replaced their Scots equivalents and were rewarded with gifts of dwellings and property in the town. Just to be on the safe side, Edward took a

Berwick, Tweedmouth and Spittal viewed from the slopes of Halidon Hill, where on 19 July 1333 the Scottish army led by Sir Archibald Douglas, Guardian of Scotland, was devastatingly defeated by Edward III. In the foreground lies the new Berwick by-pass and nearby was the Cistercian nunnery founded around 1153, as well as the now-vanished early-medieval village of Bondington (*Neil Potts*).

dozen hostages from amongst the burgesses' children who were to be held at Newcastle and York as security for good behaviour. Although there were frequent Border skirmishes, Berwick lived through an uneasy peace.

Scotland's young king and queen were now sent to safety in France and Edward Balliol performed the duties of English puppet. These included paying the promised cash for Edward III's efforts in helping him regain his inheritance, and the annexing to the English crown for ever of 'the castle, town and county of Berwick-on-Tweed'. Edward III was in Berwick during early November 1333 and he oversaw the repair of the town's mills. Now the burgh had two windmills, two horsemills and two watermills, and all of the mills as far as Edrington were inspected and repaired. Edward also took steps to remove 'dangerous' inhabitants from Berwick who were taking part in fifth-column activities.

It is not surprising then, considering Edward's attitude, that a gallows was established on Gallow's Hill, located by the present-day junction of Castle Terrace with the old A1. But there were other public ordinances too. A tolbooth and statehouse (set roughly where the modern town hall is) had already been established by 1300, and a jail supplanting the castle was set up by 1337. A separate royal residence from the castle had been established in the Palace by David I's reign, and in 1334 Edward was calling it *nostre domus* (our house).

Although Edward was much preoccupied with the Hundred Years' War, which raged sporadically between England and France from 1337 to 1453, the king did spend time at Berwick. From 1337 to 1341 trade boomed in the town, and in 1338 the burgh was favoured by a jousting match. Jousting was one of the several quasi-martial activities which had their origins in ancient Rome and was revived in northern France in the eleventh century. The word 'tournament' derives from *tournois*, the action of turning a horse to return to the lists after a charge. The organisation of such jousts was a crown prerogative, and the events were frequently bloody. It was a great compliment for Berwick to have a joust held within its liberties, and twenty Scottish knights jousted with twenty English knights at Berwick in 1338; the score was England 2 Scotland 1, the figures being fatalities.

The young king and queen of Scotland returned from France in 1341. David II was courageous enough, but his lack of experience in the arts of diplomacy and soldiering led him to an unwise alliance with the French and an invasion of England in 1346. David's army was defeated on 17 October 1346 at Neville's Cross, near Durham, and for the next eleven years he was a captive of Edward III in London and Hampshire, while in Scotland Robert the Steward carried on as Regent under the English occupation. The Scots attacked Berwick again in 1355, but the town was retaken by Edward. Probably the futility of it all led Edward III to agree to David's release under the terms of the Treaty of Berwick of 3 October 1357. Scotland was to pay 100,000 marks over ten years, the first payment beginning on the Feast of the Nativity of John the Baptist, 24 June 1358, and a truce was confirmed. The Treaty payments were always irregular and were never actually completed.

Although David II had made an inauspicious start, by the time he died at Edinburgh Castle in 1371 he was dominating his kingdom, Berwick was prosperous, and Berwick merchants had increased their wealth and influence.

David II was succeeded by his nephew, the 54-year-old Robert II, the first Stewart king. He had not the qualities of kingship, and in 1372 the Scots allied with France, which led to an inevitable war with England, and there were raids and counter-raids across the Border for most of Robert's reign. Edward III died in 1377, and early in Robert's reign the English government ordered a 'protection of burgesses' at Berwick. Even so, attacks on Berwick persisted, and in the mid-1380s John of Gaunt, Duke of Lancaster, harried the Scots as far as Edinburgh. In 1384 the Scots seized Berwick, 'betrayed into their hands for a bribe, by its deputy governor', says George Ridpath. The Scots were soon to give it up to the Duke of Lancaster on payment of 200 merks. So in the reign of Edward III Berwick Castle was twice in the hands of the Scots.

In 1388 the Douglas family took on that conflict with the Percys of Northumberland that was to be the subject of the ancient ballads *Chevy Chase* and the *Battle of Otterbourne*. These romantic excursions reflecting history give colour to Berwick society in the latter years of the fourteenth century, a time of private warfare and plague, public conflicts and pestilence. The new king of England, Richard II (1377-99), strengthened such castles as Bamburgh, and life went on for the Berwick folk in a nasty, brutish world. By 1406 Robert III of Scotland was dead and the great period of 'The Struggle for Independence', that had so affected Berwick, came to an end. Berwick welcomed the fifteenth century still firmly in English hands, but the burgh was a shadow of itself. By the mid-fourteenth century Berwick's wool trade had suffered from the Border raids—indeed every time a Border abbey was attacked Berwick suffered. This and the climatic deterioration which made the southern uplands agriculturally unviable led to local economic instability.

CHAPTER 6

Berwick Bounds, Henry's Walls and Edward's Citadel

By the fifteenth century the area of modern Railway Street and Tweed Street in Berwick had been settled as well as Foulford and Ravensdowne. Berwick harbour, too, was well advanced, the main medieval quay being from the modern boat-house, on the north bank of the Tweed, to the medieval bridge. The new century was almost actually begun by the reign of James I of Scotland, the poet, athlete and statesman, who was still an eleven-year-old child in 1406 and a prisoner of the English. All the while there were alarms along the Border and Berwick was garrisoned to the hilt by the English as an insurance against a Scottish siege which was always a threat. In 1400 Henry IV had invaded Scotland, and the Scots had looted Berwick in 1405.

James I's prospects were to improve when he fell in love with Joan Beaufort, first cousin of Henry IV, and the heroine of James's poem *The Kingis Quair* (The King's Book). By the Treaty of London in 1423, James's ransom of £40,000 was negotiated, and on 2 February 1423 he was married to Joan. They passed through Berwick on their way to Scotland and were at Melrose on 5 April 1424. James now set about the government of his kingdom, and a plethora of legislation flooded the land with laws ranging from archery to salmon fishing. Berwick's defences were strengthened in 1427. The fighting went on along the Border, the Scots under William Douglas, Earl of Angus, defeating the English under Percy and Sir Robert Ogle at Piperden, near Berwick, on 10 September 1436.

James was assassinated in the Dominican friary at Perth on 21 February 1437. One year into the reign of his successor, the six-year-old James II, the present boundaries of Berwick were established as a part of the Anglo-Scottish truce.

The idea of a fixed border between England and Scotland was more apparent than real in the fifteenth century and was

Lamberton Toll Bar

Once Lamberton Toll was as famous as Gretna Green for runaway marriages. The toll marked the northern boundary of Berwick by 1438 and was coterminous with the border between Scotland and England, fixed by royal charter in 1604. The toll cottages were demolished in 1975 to facilitate road widening.

not a legally accepted reality for another hundred years. Up to the seventeenth century the land around Berwick's boundaries was always something of a 'debateable land'. Today the term 'Borders' usually means the Scottish side of the Border line, whereas the 'English side' (a perfectly acceptable term in, say, Victorian Berwickshire) is thought of as the 'Border Country'. The chronicler Holinshed refers to the land around Berwick as the Borders in 1577, and it was probably a *de facto* term in his day.

The northern boundary of Berwick was recognised in 1438 to be coterminous with the border between Scotland and England and it began in the east, between Meg's Dub and Marshall Meadows Bay, to run south-west to join the modern A1 at the site of the old toll house, where the modern border markings are situated. Until the 1820s the main road continued over Lamberton Moor to Ayton (a main medieval road into

Scotland), and a coast road ran on to Eyemouth. Once Lamberton Toll was as famous as Gretna Green for runaway marriages, and the toll house once bore the legend, 'Ginger beer sold and marriages performed on the most reasonable terms'. An old rhyme is associated with the runaway marriages:

If a Berwick lad and lass,
Gang together by the Steps-o-Grace
They'll sup wi' the priest o'Lamberton.

The Steps-o-Grace (an allusion to the throwing off legality and godliness) is a farm still, and the 'priest', M.A.Denham tells us, referred to 'an old shoemaker, broken-down farmer, or an ousted priest', who read the English Marriage Service to anyone wishing to marry in haste; in local parlance such marriages became known as 'Buckle-the-Beggar' marriages, the 'priest' being the beggar. The last marriages were 'celebrated' by such as Henry Smith and Andrew Lyons, a tailor of Walkergate Lane, Berwick. Lamberton, as late as 1844, had about 150 marriages a year and marriages were also 'celebrated' at Paxton Toll. The cottages at Lamberton Toll associated with the runaway marriages were demolished in 1975 to facilitate road widening. Lamberton races, once held in July and August, were a great tourist attraction, and a new tourist facility complex is planned for the old toll.

Perhaps Lamberton's most famous son was William de Lamberton, Chancellor and first Bishop of Glasgow, then, during 1298-1328, Bishop of St Andrews. He was a friend of Sir William Wallace.

From medieval times the seaweed from Marshall Meadows Bay was used as fertiliser for the neighbouring fields. After the railway here was realigned away from the cliff, its old course (now a caravan park) through a disused tunnel was used for a track for trucks to be winched up from the shore full of seaweed. Above modern New East Farm is the nineteenth-century reservoir on the site of the Elizabethan Pettekar Lough which was formed by damming a burn. Nearby is the probable site of Segden, the hospital and hermitage founded by the Lindsays of Lamberton in the thirteenth century. This hospital was possibly the one moved to a site near Holy Trinity Church in the fourteenth century; its revenues were annexed to the hospital of St Mary Magdalene previous to 1437. Today the Berwick bypass joins the old Great North Road at Meadow House Inn, the first and last public house in England.

From the sea at Marshall Meadows the boundary line finalised in 1438 runs west, round the policies of Mordington House, to the crossroads on the A6105; this point is known locally as the Starch House Toll, so named after a now-vanished starch factory; when the A6105 was re-aligned in recent times at the crossroads, the old Starch House Toll houses were demolished. Here the minor Boundary Road, known by this name since the fifteenth century, meets the boundary of its junction with the turning to Low Cocklaw. To the west lies Edrington Castle in what was 'debateable land'; the castle changed hands many times and was returned to James V by Henry VIII in 1534, the land around being finally accepted as Scotland in 1603. On its rocky elevation above the Whiteadder the castle was a useful outpost for the Berwick garrison. The boundary now follows the track across the Whiteadder by ford and crosses the B6461 at Paxton Toll to meet the Tweed at Yardford (ancient Yair Ford, 'the ford by the fish trap'). This was a wild part of Berwick's extremities in medieval times, the haunt of outlaws and robbers. To the east are Berwick's 'southern boundaries' wherein are located Low Cocklaw (where a tileworks made pantiles for Berwick's houses in the eighteenth and nineteenth centuries), Baldersbury (where the coat of arms of the Corporation of Berwick is displayed), and White Damhead (which once provided power for Grangeburn Mill, a seventeenth-century mill built by the burgesses of Berwick). Between Low Cocklaw and the B6461 is New Mills (the old mills of Berwick rebuilt in 1767 and 1873), and across the Whiteadder is Gainslaw House, once the home of the Comptons who were prominent in eighteenth-century Berwick. At Gainslaw the Duke of Norfolk encamped in 1542 during an unsuccessful raid into Scotland. Further east is Whiteadder Bridge (known locally as Canties Bridge) of 1973 which replaces the bridge of 1867-8, destroyed in the 1948 flood.

From the ford the boundary follows the Tweed to the North Sea. By the fixing of the 1438 boundary much more territory was ceded to Berwick, for in the early fourteenth century the boundary of Berwick was considered only to extend across the neck of the town peninsula from sea to river just a short distance north of the medieval walls. The boundary of 1438 was more firmly fixed by 1604. The land within the boundary, called the 'Liberties of Berwick', was, from James VI & I's time (his charter of 30 April 1603), leased to individuals, and the revenues were used for the 'support of the Municipal Establishment of the Borough', and the residue of land was divided amongst 'the senior resident burgesses, or their widows'. The burgesses dug ditches and set up cairns to indicate where their land began and ended. The land was called 'stints' and these were small strips or portions of arable land which the burgesses used themselves or leased out. The area of the modern Meadows is within the old stints.

It was not until 1542 that it was noted that the boundaries were being regularly perambulated, and in 1550 it was recommended that the town garrison patrol this border regularly. This was purely a military patrol, but from 1609 onwards the mayor and corporation rode the bounds. The traditional Riding of the Bounds ceremony is still enacted on 1st May, and while the civic party travel by bus, a group of riders assemble at the Parade to ride off to the bounds.

On the death of James I in 1437, Archibald, 5th Earl of Douglas, was appointed Regent of Scotland during the minority of James II and there was to be continual jockeying amongst the Scottish nobility to control the royal minor. The period was one of raid and counter-raid amongst the Scottish landowners with further Border disturbances; during 16-22 August 1455 James II invaded England and made an abortive attack on Berwick. The years 1455 to 1460 were spent in Scotland with a consolidation of royal power, and while England was involved in the early years of the Wars of the Roses

(1455-85), the Scots recaptured Roxburgh. While the walls of Roxburgh were being bombarded, James II was killed by an exploding cannon on 3 August 1460. The nine-year-old James III now ascended the throne of Scotland and government was enacted through the statesman-priest James Kennedy, Bishop of St Andrews, who favoured the Lancastrian side against the Yorkist in the Wars of the Roses. Asylum was granted to the Lancastrian king Henry VI and his wife Margaret of Anjou, and in 1461, when Henry VI was escaping to Scotland, he gave Berwick to the Scots. The young James III visited Berwick on 15 June 1461 and the Scots made an effort to repair its defences; alas, the town was destitute, although courts were held there and administration carried on. In 1478-79 the *Scottish Exchequer Rolls* were recording that even the farms of the burgh were irrecoverable through neglect.

In 1482 the now free Duke of Albany—James III's brother whom he had imprisoned—invaded Scotland accompanied by the Yorkist Richard, Duke of Gloucester. Gloucester took Berwick in this year and the town never again changed hands. During 1482-88 there were various phases of extensive repairs to its walls, largely under the supervision of William Tyler, the Captain. 'Tyler's Stone Bulwark in the Sands' is one piece of prominent construction of the period; this was a square-towered seaward military defence wrapped around a medieval tower (of which the modern site is Coxon's Tower).

On 30 July 1503 there arrived at Berwick, to a welcoming cannonade from the castle and the town walls, Margaret Tudor, daughter of Henry VII, bound for Scotland and her nuptials with James IV, who had succeeded James III after the latter's assassination in 1488. Two days later she and her entourage of eighteen hundred knights and ladies, led by the Earls of Surrey and Northumberland, made their slow progress to the rendezvous at Lamberton church. Her palfrey guided by Sir Thomas Worteley, her master of horse, Margaret was brought to the pavilions set up by the church and given over into the care of the thousand-strong Scots retinue. Margaret was received by the Archbishop of Glasgow who, after she had supped, took her and five hundred of her suite to Coldingham Priory for that evening. Next morning the English princess set off to Dunbar and Dalkeith and on 8 August 1503 she became Queen of Scots.

From 1488 until 1512 Scotland had a technical peace with England, save for the Scots support of the pretender Perkin Warbeck against Henry VII, and even although there was an undeclared naval war from 1504. The Holy League of 1511, formed by Pope Julius II, to oppose the expansionist policy of Louis XII of France, was joined by Henry VIII who now put aside thoughts of his border with Scotland to foray in France. Louis invoked Scotland's traditional, and recently renewed, 'auld alliance' with his nation and encouraged James IV to tie up England's troops by a northern diversion.

By mid-July 1513 urgent messages were sent to London from Berwick reporting that all along the south-east Borders, the Scots were removing their goods and cattle—a sure sign of impending conflict. Berwick's citizens urgently asked for money to repair their fortifications. On 22 August 1513 the Scottish army crossed the Tweed near Coldstream and set up their banners on English soil. Although the surrounding castles of Etal, Ford and Norham were taken, Berwick was not attacked. At Flodden Hill the 40,000-strong Scots army faced the 26,000 troops and cavalry led by the 70 year-old Thomas Howard, Earl of Surrey, Lieutenant General of the North of England. Berwick played no direct part in the battle.

The Battle of Flodden was a bloody massacre in which the Scots lost their king, most of their nobility, gentry and administrative class. James IV's naked corpse was soon identified by Lord Dacre, Captain of Berwick, and after lying for the night at Branxton Church it was carried to Berwick with the captured Scottish artillery. The embalmed body was handed over to Lord Norfolk and taken to London where it was to remain for several years unburied to end up in a lumber room at Sheen Palace; later the Scots king's head was buried in an unmarked grave at St Michael's Cornhill, London. The Scottish artillery was taken to the Maison Dieu quay at Berwick to be shipped to the Tower.

Lying to the south of Northumberland Avenue, the Bell Tower of *circa* 1576, with its medieval base, stands proud on the ruined Edwardian walls. Nearby were the now-vanished Dominican and Franciscan friaries famous in the town's ecclesiastical history. In the foreground is Lord's Mount, a distinctive artillery fort of 1539-42, said to have been designed by Henry VIII himself. Excavated during 1972-73, the emergent fort exhibits gun emplacements, fireplaces, an oven, a well and a privy (*Neil Potts*).

The one-year-old James V now ascended the throne and Scotland was once more troubled by those problems brought about by a regency for an infant monarch. In 1515 John Stewart, Duke of Albany, replaced Queen Margaret (she had married the Earl of Angus in 1514) as Regent. Albany twice led an army to the Scottish border during 1522-23, but the memory of Flodden led to no more than huffing and puffing. On 10 October 1526 a truce was signed at Berwick, which languished except for a few incursions from her castle into Scotland for plunder and ravaging of villages; there was little action until the 'King's Great Works' on the town's fortifications.

The reigns of Henry VIII, Edward VI and Mary I—the period 1509 to 1588—saw great building plans in Berwick as a curtain-raiser to the reconstruction of the medieval defences in Elizabeth I's reign.

The sixteenth-century repairs started in earnest on 12 December 1508 when Henry VII engaged William, Lord Conyers, as Captain of Berwick to supervise renovations. The chain of command began with the Privy Council to whom the Captain had to answer. Under him was the Surveyor or Clerk of Works, with a Master Mason at 8d a day and a Master Carpenter at 1s.6d a day. It must be said that some of the higher administrative positions were sinecures and not *in situ* appointments, and interest at London in the work going on in Berwick usually only revived when the Scots were a threat. For the new works the Crown supplied twenty-five craftsmen, whom the Captain had to match with twenty-five labourers, and there was much embezzlement and fraud. Timber came from Newcastle, Bladon and Essex, and locally quarried limestone was used with bricks from Hull. Henry VIII's great works came in three phases: the erection of gun towers at the White Walls; the construction of Lord's Mount, also called Henry's Citadel; and the great earthwork before the salient in the east town wall.

The development of artillery in the sixteenth century ended the effectiveness of the traditional medieval fortifications of high walls and flanking towers, and by the mid-sixteenth century Berwick's fortifications were a blend of medieval work and piecemeal improvements. Consequently by the reign of Henry VIII the restructuring of Berwick's fortifications was absolutely necessary as they were dilapidated and virtually useless.

The most important part of the Henrician construction was that known as Lord's Mount, built in 1539-42 to succeed the earthen bulwark of 1522-23. The defence is a circular tower of about 100ft diameter which was meant to be self-sufficient. Excavation during 1972-73 showed the two-level gun emplacements for six guns, fireplaces, an oven, a privy, a well and a magazine. Probably two types of gun were used: on the top deck, culverines on heavy carriages, and below, the iron breach-loaded serpentine on a swivel mount. It is known that the military engineer Stefan van Haschenperg did some work on Henry's walls, although it is said that the king himself designed the bastion. In all probability muzzle-loaders of brass would be used on the rebuilt walls.

During Edward VI's reign major improvements were planned with the erection of a citadel to lie athwart the medieval wall to the east. Work was begun on the square bastioned citadel in 1548 and the work proceeded slowly. Even by the end of Mary's reign in 1558 the second-stage work by William Ridgeway was still incomplete, and the whole was totally obsolete.

In 1544-45 Berwick saw something of the notorious campaigns of the 'Rough Wooing', which were part of Henry VIII's scheme to have his son Edward marry the infant Mary, Queen of Scots. The devastation wrought in Scotland included the destruction of the Border abbeys and many a town and village was put to the torch.

During 1549-51 Berwick played host to one of the main protagonists of Scotland's Reformation. John Knox was born around 1514 at Giffordgate, Haddington, and was educated at the local grammar school and at the University of St Andrews. Almost nothing is known of his life until he became a priest, and between 1540 and 1543 he acted as an ecclesiastical notary of the diocese of St Andrews. In 1546 he attached himself to the Protestant preacher George Wishart who was executed the same year at St Andrews for heresy. Knox joined the murderers of Cardinal David Beaton, Archbishop of St Andrews—who had ordered Wishart's immolation—in St Andrews Castle in 1547. But when the castle fell to a Franco-Scottish expedition he was shipped to the French prison galleys. Under the terms of a peace treaty of 1549, he was released and made his way to the Protestant England of Edward VI.

Soon after his arrival, the Privy Council appointed Knox as chaplain to Berwick Parish Church. Berwick in the mid-sixteenth century was clogged with garbage and human filth and was poverty-stricken. Society was violent, and whenever foreign mercenaries passed through the town there was an upsurge of looting, rape and murder. The population of the town was around 3500 in Knox's time, of whom about 1000 were soldiers or workmen associated with the fortifications and garrison. Indeed, because of the turbulence of the time, Berwick's garrison had been increased by 200 foot soldiers and 100 cavalry. Men outnumbered women four to one. The town was the headquarters of the Lord Warden of the East Marches; the military personnel were the responsibility of the Marshal of Berwick and the civilians answered to the Mayor, but the Lord Warden had the final say in all matters. The soldiery were a discontented lot; they hated Berwick as it was cold, wet and windy, and worse, their pay was always in arrears.

Knox himself was not unpopular; as a Scot he was better liked by some than the English, for many sixteenth-century Berwick folk were of Scots origin. The town teemed with illegal Scottish immigrants who regularly crossed the Border to take advantage of the exchange rates—the English pound could buy £5.14s.0d of Scottish goods. Scots were viewed with suspicion by the authorities, and any Scot lurking near the castle or fortifications after curfew would be executed.   A preacher in Berwick had to be tough. Around the mid-1540s John Brende, writing to his superior the Lord Protector Edward Seymour, Duke of Somerset, said: 'There is better order among the Tartars than in Berwick...no man can have anything unstolen'. Relations between the burgesses and the military were often acrimonious and morale was low. Knox's preaching seems to have had some effect. Writing of his parish ministry at Berwick, and answering a complaint by Mary, Queen of Scots, about the inflammatory nature of his preaching, he said: 'I shame not, Madam, further to affirm that God so blessed my weak labours that in Berwick— where commonly before there used to be slaughter by reason of quarrels arising among the soldiers—there was as great quietness all the time I remained there as there is this day in Edinburgh'. So all in all it seems that Knox was a wise choice by the Privy Council. He had had experience of the unruly garrison at St Andrews in 1547 and he was a Scot among a large assembly of Scots.

Knox propagated the Reformed doctrine in Berwick; he sowed some of the early seeds of English Puritanism; he introduced forms of worship distinctly Puritan in character; he eschewed the old communion and promoted the 'sitting down' variety of worship. And always he attacked the mass in his sermons and promoted the Zwinglian doctrine of the Lord's Supper (a denial of the Real Presence of Christ in the bread and wine in the Sacrament of the Altar).

In all these things he earned the hostility of Cuthbert Tunstall, the conservative Bishop of Durham—Berwick was now within the diocese of Durham—and Knox was summoned from Berwick to defend his doctrines before the Council of the North at Newcastle. His speech was later published as *A Vindication of the Doctrine that the Sacrifice of the Mass is Idolatry* (1556). His attitudes were those which were gathering popularity, so Tunstall took no action and returned Knox to Berwick.

Knox did show caution when it came to dealing with the immorality and corruption which were rampant in sixteenth-century Berwick. As a government agent he had the right to preach against adultery, fornication, dicing, swearing, and flamboyant clothing. At Berwick the garrison were actively forbidden to play cards (except during the twenty days at Christmas) under pain of three days' imprisonment and the forfeiture of all winnings which were to go to the fund to repair Berwick's dilapidated wooden bridge and to build a new church. Knox knew that the Lord Warden of the East Marches, Henry Manners, Earl of Rutland, played cards with his officers every evening at the castle and that he paid for his losses out of the bridge and church fund. So it was politic to rail only in general terms against the greed and oppression of the upper classes. Knox was after all a Scots refugee who was lately sprung by the English from a French prison. Still, his Berwick sermons were noted in Scotland and many came from the Berwickshire towns to hear him preach—some even set up home in Berwick to be part of his congregation. Knox's Berwick sermons were to become celebrated and he published two 'letters' to his flock as *A Godly Letter of Warning or Admonition to the Faithful in London, Newcastle and Berwick* (1554), and *An Epistle to the Inhabitants of Newcastle and Berwick* (1588).

In 1551 Knox was removed by the Privy Council to the parish church of St Nicholas at Newcastle, to assist the vicar, William Purye, but he returned the long day's ride to Berwick frequently to preach and celebrate his form of communion. During this year Berwick entertained the Scots Queen Mother, Marie de Guise-Lorraine, on her way home from a visit to France. Soon Knox was to be a celebrated enemy of her unfortunate daughter.

Knox met in Berwick many zealous Protestants within an environment which was Catholic, and one meeting was to alter his life personally. Among his Berwick congregation was Mrs Elizabeth Bowes, the wife of Richard Bowes, Captain of Norham Castle. One of her ten children was Marjorie, whose brother was Sir George Bowes, Knight Marshal of Berwick; Knox married Marjorie Bowes on 25 May 1552 (or 1553).

With the accession of the Catholic Mary Tudor in England the population of Berwick was temporarily swollen as Protestants made their way into Scotland. In the northern kingdom some like John Hamilton, Archbishop of St Andrews, were trying to reform the medieval church. But the die was cast; the ill-judged burning of the octogenarian apostate priest and heretic Walter Myln at St Andrews in the year of Elizabeth I's accession (1558) accelerated the iconoclastic riots. Civil war was in the air and Berwick stood reluctant witness to events which would bring her once more to the centre of the stage.

CHAPTER 7

Elizabethan Berwick

Elizabeth Tudor, born at the riverside palace of Greenwich on 7 September 1533, the daughter of Henry VIII and Anne Boleyn, succeeded her Roman Catholic sister Mary I to the throne of England on 17 November 1558. Although England was still at war with France, Elizabeth's was a peaceful accession and she was to herald a new age; and Berwick was to see the greatest building programme in its history.

Although there were no French mercenaries at Berwick during the mid-sixteenth century, there was a French presence nearby. The English had established a fort on the promontory above Eyemouth in 1547 and they had stayed there until 1550 when it was demolished according to the Treaty of Boulogne. To this fort came the French General D'Oysel in 1557 to rebuild the defences as a part of the Franco-Scottish campaign against the English. To thwart the building of the fort patrols regularly left Berwick to harry the work; Eyemouth's grain mill and stores were a prime target for the English. There were corresponding reprisals. For instance in 1558 harvesters were working on Halidon Hill, guarded by Berwick garrison troops, when they were attacked by French from Eyemouth. With a patrol from Berwick, Sir James Croft saw them off.

The English were always anxious about the French presence in Scotland, and it was because of the French that Berwick achieved international importance. On 27 February 1560 the Treaty of Berwick was signed in the town by Lord James Stewart and Lord William Ruthven, creating an alliance between England and the Protestant Scottish Lords of the Congregation to expel the French, who were helping the Regent Marie de Guise-Lorraine against the Calvinists. Mary Stuart was to remain Queen of Scotland by the Treaty, although she had insulted Elizabeth by using her English title. The French were driven back into Leith and they agreed to depart under the terms of the Treaty of Edinburgh of July 1560.

In the sixteenth century, Berwick—often referred to as 'a towne of warre'—was sandwiched between the Scottish East March, which stretched from Lauder and Hume Castle in the west to Fast Castle and Eyemouth Fort in the east, and the English East March with its strongholds of Wark, Etal, Ford and Norham.

Elizabethan Berwick was the administrative centre of the East March. The governorship of the castle and the Wardenship of the East March were now a combined role. During this time the castle was increasingly used as a prison for the more dangerous and important of the Border offenders. People like Sir Walter Scott of Buccleuch and Sir Robert Ker, the wardens of the Scottish Marches, incarcerated for not giving up certain prisoners, and Thomas Percy, Earl of Northumberland, an aristocratic guerrilla the costs of whose imprisonment amounted to £109. The Elizabethan garrison at Berwick was administered by the Lord Governor, the Marshal (a kind of deputy governor), the Treasurer and Victualler, the Gentleman Porter and the Master of Ordnance. All the top men had to be versed in diplomatic matters. The garrison itself was made up of eight constables, eighty horsemen, eight captains and five hundred men, and a master gunner and seventy gunners, to say nothing of a multitude of grooms, clerks and lackeys. The upkeep of the Berwick garrison cost Elizabeth some £14,860 per year.

The position of governor of Berwick was an important one, and from 1568 to 1596 it was held by the queen's first cousin Henry Carey, first Lord Hunsdon (c.1524-96). In 1564 there occurs the very first notice of an incoming governor to the town in the Guild Books.

From the accounts of one of the Elizabethan Treasurer-Victuallers, Sir Valentine Browne, who served from 1566 to 1576, we see something of the catering needs of the garrison. He had to keep to hand foodstuffs for 1500 persons, and the daily ration of the soldiery was a penny loaf (24oz of bread), a penny bottle of beer, half a pound of butter, a pound of cheese

The Elizabethan masonry of Cumberland Bastion remains as a fine example of the ramparts planned for Berwick by the military engineer Sir Richard Lee in 1558. Named after William Augustus, Duke of Cumberland, the victor of Culloden in 1746, the bastion was once called Middle Mount and is built of stone and filled with earth; once the walls had a now filled-in continuous sentry path and the moat was flooded with water (*Neil Potts*).

and two pounds of beef or mutton. Provisions were brought from as far away as Lynn. A strain was always put on supplies during times of crisis or when armies were sent via Berwick. Money was always short for victuals and to pay men.

Elizabethan Berwick was always in a state of constant alert, particularly at times of politico-religious crises like the Massacre of St Bartholomew in Paris when on 24 August 1572, over two thousand Huguenots, men, women and children, were exterminated with horrific brutality by the order of the Roman Catholic Court. The Spanish Armada also raised alarms in Berwick. The English were always afraid that the Catholic French, or indeed the Spanish, would invade across the vulnerable Border. Berwick, however, had nothing to fear from the Armada, for on 11 August 1588, dogged by the

English fleet, it sailed past the mouth of the Tweed.

Elizabethan Berwick was the usual route into Scotland, and most of the Privy Council passports were issued for Berwick. The movements of people and goods in and out of the town were all reported back to Elizabeth I's Secretary of State and new Lord High Treasurer, William Cecil, 1st Baron Burleigh (1520-98). Indeed sixteenth-century Berwick was the equivalent of Lisbon in the 1930s and 1940s; it was a place where spies gathered, it was a town of intrigue, of ministers who fled from James's establishment of episcopacy in Scotland, and of exiled lords who plotted their return to Scotland. Berwick was the centre for the organisation of the English secret service in Scotland. The governor employed, paid and interviewed informers and spies from Scotland on a regular basis. All the correspondence of the foreign ambassadors (particularly the French) was monitored at Berwick and the governor arranged for the safe despatch to London of reports by the English ambassador to the Scottish Court. Money to bribe Scots gentry was channelled through Berwick. One document has survived which gives an example of the surveillance that went on in Berwick, not least of the administrators themselves. In 1587 Henry, Earl of Huntingdon, Lord President of the Council in the North, received from one Robert Ardern, Collector of Customs, a confidential report on Berwick and its environs. In the report Ardern cites the deputy governor, Sir Henry Widdrington, as a security risk because he was 'utterly unable' to carry out his duties because of the unjust nature of his character and his scheming ways. He was allowing letters, money, books and documents to pass through Berwick without check. This was a grave dereliction of duty as the Northumberland gentry around Berwick were plotting papists.

By Elizabeth's reign, Berwick had a totally obsolete defence system which had looked even more vulnerable when England's only other outpost, Calais, had fallen to the French on 7 January 1558 in the closing months of Mary Tudor's reign. For a while the French king had been urging the Scots to attack England, so it was increasingly necessary to re-fortify Berwick.

A portion of Windmill Bastion on the Elizabethan Walls overlooks the remains of Edward VI's 'citadel' of 1551-57. The bastion still retains the nineteenth-century gun mounts once an important part of local coastal defence. Here was sited a windmill by 1587. In the distance lies the pier of 1800-21; Queen Elizabeth's Pier was built in 1577 to replace the medieval breakwater known as Holdman Wall. The lighthouse dates from 1826 (*Neil Potts*).

The earliest description of Berwick's fortifications is in the antiquarian William Camden's *Britannia* (1586), and the first account based on State Papers is by George Ridpath in his *Border History* (1776).

In January 1558 the celebrated English military engineer, Sir Richard Lee, travelled to Berwick and new building was commenced. The new schemes had been planned and begun in Mary Tudor's reign, but the bulk of the work is Elizabethan. The whole was built by Sir Richard Lee and his master mason, Rowland Johnson. Their system was one which had been developed in Italy to ensure towns had better protection against gunfire.

There were huge projecting bastions, shaped like foreshortened arrowheads, built of stone and filled with earth, joined by a sturdy curtain wall also backed with earth. The original infill was rubble taken from the medieval walls supplemented with stone from the seashore. The bastions, the equivalent of the towers of a medieval castle, were used as platforms for guns with an all-round field of fire. This ensured that Berwick was now adequately protected from an enemy approaching its most vulnerable areas to north and east. Each bastion offered its neighbour covering fire. Around the bastions and the curtain walls was a 20ft-wide trench; in the middle of this was an 8ft-deep and 12ft-wide ditch permanently filled with water. The moats have long since been filled in with the developments around the foot of the walls. With this new construction the old castle and medieval walls were abandoned, all overshadowed by the new bastions of Meg's Mount, Cumberland Bastion, Brass Bastion, Windmill Bastion and King's Mount. As the building proceeded compromises and alterations were carried out from the original concept. In 1560 an Italian engineer, Giovanni Portinari, was called in to advise, although his advice (to fortify the whole peninsula on which Berwick stands), backed up by another distinguished Italian engineer, Jacopo A'Contio, was ignored. By 1561 over one thousand men were working on the project, and by 1565 or so the new walls were in a defensible condition. Work more or less came to an end, with the construction unfinished, soon after 1566. This was ostensibly because the final defeat of Mary, Queen of Scots at Langside and her flight into England to eighteen years of imprisonment in 1569, and the suspension of Franco-Scottish collaboration, all reduced the danger of invasion. The fortifications at Berwick were the costliest building programme of Elizabeth's reign at some £9,900 per annum.

The Elizabethan Walls can be examined in detail on foot. A good place to start is by mounting the walls at the Scotsgate as it crosses the old A1 (Great North Road) out of Berwick. The walls are in the care of English Heritage. Originally there were four gates into Berwick: Nessgate (or Piergate) overlooking the river to the south; Bridgegate (or Englishgate, renovated in 1816 and removed in 1825) by the Old Bridge; Shoregate (Sandgate); and Cowgate (Cowport). Scotsgate was completed in stone in 1590 and was called New Gate, or New Mary Gate; it was altered in 1815-16 and renovated in 1858. A side arch was added at the same time. Scotsgate had its own bridge across the moat and guardhouse at the foot of the still extant stairs. Incidentally just outside the Scotsgate, where the car park and modern Information Centre are now located, was the church of St Mary, pulled down to make way for the fortifications; the church gave its name to the gateway and to the road leading down into the burgh. On the site of the modern car park was the cattle market of 1886.

At the western extremity of this section of the Elizabethan Walls, to the left of the Scotsgate, lies the unfinished Meg's Mount. It received its name of Roaring Meg's Mount from the gun which was placed on it; it was also called West Mount in past days. The fortification is a demi-bastion with one flanker facing east and was begun in 1558, work proceeding eastwards. A flanker, by the by, is a gun emplacement in the flank of a bastion. The paths around the ramparts were laid out in 1837. The masonry walls of all the bastions are twenty feet high with long orillons ('ears') to protect the flanking emplacements. Around the bastions, but behind the flankers, runs a (now filled-in) cobbled sentry-path, and above this the parapet. The guns were later set on cavaliers, the name for their platform. Indeed the present ramparts and cavaliers are of Civil War date or later. To the south Meg's Mount overlooks Bankhill and the monument to Lady Jerningham, wife of Sir Hubert Jerningham, MP, of Longridge Towers. Four years after her death in 1902 Jerningham, who had designed the memorial himself, had it sculpted by O.P.Penachini. Down the steep path to the New Road (under the Royal Tweed Bridge) lies an early nineteenth-century icehouse which was used to store ice to preserve the salmon to be shipped to London and elsewhere; the ice was collected from local ponds or imported from Norway.

The next bastion to Meg's is Cumberland (once Middle

Mount), renamed after HRH William Augustus, Duke of Cumberland (1721-65), the victor of Culloden in 1746. Cumberland passed through Berwick on his way to the battle. This is a full bastion with flankers to east and west reached by tunnels through the ramparts. A late seventeenth-century gun, on a replica gun carriage, adds some historical atmosphere to the flanker. Houses to the north of the bastion were removed in 1715 to enhance the fire range from the ramparts. The basic work is Elizabethan, but with earthworks dating from 1639-53, and the upper parts were reconstructed during 1690-1715. The linking wall between Cumberland Bastion and Brass Bastion cuts off the street now made a *cul-de-sac* at Wallace Green; this street led originally into Low Greens and a gateway with bridge and moat was once intended here.

Brass Bastion (formerly Brass Mount and Bedford Mount after Francis Russell, 2nd Earl of Bedford, governor of Berwick, 1562-68) is the north-east corner of the Elizabethan defences. It takes its name from a brass cannon which was mounted here. The earthwork was also known as Search House Bastion, because the search watch (which patrolled the walls) had a guardroom here. From the Brass Bastion the Covered Way was dug in May 1565 by three hundred men working full day shifts; this served as an obstacle to an enemy trying to cross the fields, and it was a safe route for soldiers going across to the cliffs. Here can be seen a section of the original sentry walk, and the flankers are reached by tunnels through the earthwork. Below the Brass Bastion was the Elizabethan Batardeau, a dam which controlled the level of the water in the moat at the north side of the ramparts. Along the east stretch of the curtain wall from Brass Bastion runs the Stanks (being the Scottish word for ditches), now a playingfield. In this east wall is the Cowport, or Cowgate, built 1595-6 and then called Carey Port (after the family name of the Hunsdons); there was an earlier wooden gateway in the Edwardian Wall here. Through this gateway the townsfolk led their cattle to graze. The portcullis slot is still to be seen and the wooden doors date from around 1750 and were renovated 1979-80.

Behind Windmill Mount, on Berwick's Elizabethan walls, lies the early nineteenth-century Lions House, restored in recent times. The Lions Gardens, on the left, are used as allotments these days, but lie in the moat of the Edward VI 'citadel'. To the right, behind its own retaining wall, is the vaulted and buttressed magazine of 1749, which was built to replace the damp armoury magazine set in the flankers of Brass Bastion (*Neil Potts*).

The Windmill Mount (once Milne Mount) is a regular bastion and there was a windmill on it from about 1587. Probably this windmill, and others in the town, came ready-made from Ghent. The gun platforms are of the nineteenth century and were set up as a part of a coastal defence. Guns were manned here by the 1st Berwick Artillery Volunteers until 1908, and there were anti-aircraft guns here during World War II. The Great Bulwark in the Snook lies to the east, and the Elizabethan Wall crosses the site of the old Edwardian Citadel as the curtain wall drives south to King's Mount. King's Mount was once called St Nicholas Mount after a medieval church which stood here (see page 39). Then it was Hunsdon's New Mount after the governor, and it probably changed its name again in 1603 when James VI & I came to the town. The fortification is demi-bastion with the cavalier removed.

D

At King's Mount the Elizabethan fortifications join the medieval town wall, which from here to Meg's Mount was substantially rebuilt in the eighteenth century. This stretch is properly called the Georgian Walls and is dealt with on pages 112 and 113. This sixteenth-century idea had been to cut off what was known as the Lower Town (modern Palace Green) and link King's Mount roughly with Meg's Mount. Work on such a fortified line, known on old maps as the Catwell Wall, was begun 1561-62, but abandoned soon after. Indeed the royal storehouses in the region of the harbour in the Lower Town (near modern Coxon's Tower) were to have been secured in another alternative plan, but this too was abandoned. Today there is no trace of the Catwell Wall, which would have linked the salient angles of Meg's Mount and King's Mount. It took its name from the healing well situated at the foot of Hide Hill, where Burrell's Tower stood to protect entry at this point.

It is ironic that in the year that the work on the Elizabethan Walls came to an end (1566) Mary, Queen of Scots, whose activities made the wall a necessity, came to view Berwick on her way from Jedburgh. She was met at the Bound Road by Sir John Forrester, the deputy governor, and was taken to Halidon Hill to view the town. As she sat on horseback on this elevation, she was saluted by the cannon on the new walls; exactly twenty-two years later her son James would be saluted in the same way; but James was not a threat. In 1586 a treaty of 'straiter friendship' had been agreed at Berwick in which Edward, Earl of Rutland, representing Elizabeth, and Francis, Earl of Bothwell, representing James VI, had assured 'truce and peace' in the south-east Borders.

When the Elizabethan Walls were built they excluded around a third of the town to the north. The area known as Castlegate and the Greenses (High Greens and Low Greens) were still enclosed by the defunct medieval walls, but were not entirely built on by the sixteenth century. The area only developed in the nineteenth century when it became the quarter of the fishing community.

By the year 1576 the condition of Berwick haven was causing

trouble again, and the master mason engineer since 1567, Rowland Johnson, gave advice on the construction of a stone pier. When work began in 1577, it was the design of Berwick's master gunner, John Fleming, which was used. The pier ran to a length of 1077 feet and was 22 feet thick; its remains were still visible when a new pier was built in 1810-21.

By the time Lord Willoughby de Eresby took over as governor in 1598, Berwick was militarily almost useless, indeed the town was not politically important. The Scots were scornful of Berwick's fortifications and by 1601 were boasting that they 'could take Berwick any market day'; happily come the death of Elizabeth I in 1603 Berwick had no need to defend herself.

CHAPTER 8

Under Stuart and Commonwealth

On 26 March 1603, James Stuart was proclaimed at Berwick, King of England, France and Ireland, by the name of James VI & I. On this occasion, however, James, without the consent of Parliament, adopted the title of 'King of Great Britain'. The news of Elizabeth I's death had caused some unruly behaviour in the south-east Borders, but this was quelled by the deputies of Sir Robert Carey, Warden of the Middle March, and James now made the long journey south with a retinue of five hundred to take up his inheritance. On his arrival at the Berwick boundary he was received by Sir John Carey, the marshal, along with the officers of the Berwick garrison. James's way had been paved by his representative John Bothwell, Commendator and Lord Abbot of Holyrood, whom he had sent to take over the town. James passed through a welcoming volley of discharging muskets and was saluted by a cannonade from the ramparts of Elizabeth's Walls. As he entered the town the keys of Berwick were delivered to him by the Gentleman Porter, William Selby, who received a knighthood (conferred on the spot) from the king. Through the armed bands of the garrison, James rode into the market place to receive the 'body corporate of the borough' and Hugh Gregson, the mayor, presented him with a gift of gold and surrendered the town's charter. Christopher Parkinson, the Recorder of Berwick, then addressed the king with a solemn congratulatory speech. Symbolically James restored the charter, thus assuring the town of his royal favour and protection of its rights. After this ceremony the king proceeded to the old parish church to give thanks for his peaceful entry into his new dual kingdom, and Toby Matthew, Bishop of Durham, preached a sermon. On coming out of church again, King James acknowledged the cheers of the crowd and visited the castle.

Holy Trinity Church, drawn by the Berwick artist Thomas Sword Good (1739-1872) and engraved by Robert Scott (1777-1841) of Edinburgh for the Rev. Thomas Johnstone's *The History of Berwick-upon-Tweed and Vicinity* (1817). The west front of the church shows the pre-1855 west window and the former simpler design. In these days the churchyard was treeless.

James's charter for Berwick was confirmed in 1604 and the rights therein included: the making of Berwick a 'free borough for ever'; powers to make laws 'for the good of the borough'; enablement to elect a mayor (from the burgesses) annually at Michaelmas; power to elect four bailiffs a year and a recorder; the mayor, bailiffs and recorder to hold a borough court fortnightly, and to have the right to choose a coroner and have four Sergeants at Mace to serve the court; and to have a merchant guild. The charter also granted a fair.

There had been fairs and markets in Berwick, of course, long before this. It is interesting to note that the Calf Hill behind the Toll House at the junction of the Great North Road and the A6105 (where Alva Lodge stands today) was an Elizabethan market for the Scots who were excluded from the town after

1560. In James's charter the fair was specified as: from the Feast of the Finding of the Holy Cross (3 May) to the Feast of the Nativity of St John the Baptist (24 June); this confirmed a similar grant by Edward I in 1302. There were to be five markets at Berwick, two held weekly on Wednesdays and Saturdays and three 'High Markets' for the sale of black cattle, horses and for the hiring of servants; these were held on the second Wednesday of May, the Wednesday preceding 26 August and the first Wednesday of November. An Annual Fair was held during the Friday of Trinity Week.

The day after his arrival at Berwick, James received obeisance from the gentry of north Northumberland and further south and inspected the town's fortifications, port and magazines, during which he himself fired one of the great guns. That day word was brought to him that certain *banditti* had rioted and pillaged from Carlisle to Penrith; James despatched Sir William Selby to quell the rioters. James continued his journey to London the next day and soon after his arrival in London he ordered the dissolution of the garrison at Berwick: it continued, though, as a company of one hundred infantrymen under a captain. The governorship was already in abeyance following the death of Lord Willoughby in 1601. As a part of his policy of reconciliation between his two nations along the Border, James prohibited the term 'the Borders' being used and substituted 'The Middle Shires'. The historian Ridpath tells us: 'He ordered all the places of strength in these parts to be demolished, except the habitations of noblemen and barons; their iron gates to be converted into ploughshares and the inhabitants to betake themselves to agriculture and the other works of peace'.

Within the town the mayor and commonalty took over the crown buildings including the palace and its appurtenances, Burrell's Tower, the Governor's House, the Maison Dieu and all buildings not of a military use. Soon the burgesses were to fly the new flag of Great Britain, the first Union Jack with the combined crosses of St Andrew and St George (the cross of St Patrick was not added until 1801).

During the whole of James VI & I's reign Berwick was neglected, but the seventeenth century did produce two significant structures, a new bridge (known today as the 'Old Bridge') and a new parish church.

Up to 1603 there were four known road bridges over the Tweed at Berwick, but as they were always in a poor state of repair, ferries and fords flourished from early times. The first of the medieval bridges is referred to in the reign of Malcolm IV of Scotland (1153-65), but it was destroyed by the flood of 1199. Roger Hoveden in his *Chronica* tells us of this and how the bridge was repaired by Earl Patrick, Warden of Berwick, with the reluctant permission of Philip, Bishop of Durham, who owned the Tweedmouth shore. A timber bridge on a stone foundation was built soon after and it suffered damage by King John in 1216; whatever was left of this bridge and any subsequent rebuilding to represent a third phase was badly damaged again by a flood on the Feast of St Peter ad Vincula, 1 August 1294, the *Lanercost Chronicle* tells us; and for some two hundred years Berwick had no passable bridge. Henry VII is credited with having a wooden bridge built in the fifteenth century, and this had a stone tower towards the Tweedmouth end.

A new bridge for Berwick had been talked about since 1564 when the fortifications were being assessed, but new impetus was engendered by George Home, Earl of Dunbar, James VI & I's adviser on Scottish affairs. It would be the symbol of the union of the crowns, Dunbar emphasised; the king liked the idea and resurrected the office of Governor of Berwick for Dunbar, who became the chief agent in the bridge's construction.

The Berwick mason chiefly responsible for the bridge was the Surveyor and Berwick guildsman, James Burrell, who was to be mayor of the town from 1609-11. The repair of the fifteenth-century bridge was put in hand—the job was halted when floating ice damaged the fabric in 1607-08—but a ferry eased the passage across the Tweed. This episode assisted the lobby which wanted a new stone bridge. Despite the blow of the death of the bridge's main supporter, the Earl of Dunbar, in 1611, money was collected and work commenced on 19 June 1611.

Stone from the quarry at Tweedmouth was used mainly and work proceeded steadily though funds remained tight. The work began to slow down through delays in late delivery of supplies and flooding. The construction was now inspected by the king's new agent, Richard Neile, Bishop of Durham, who devised new work schedules and estimates of future cost; he calculated that the bridge would be ready for vehicles by the midsummer of 1621. The bishop now engaged the Newcastle bridge master John Johnston to supervise the work which now proceeded rapidly; but disaster struck again in 1621 with exceptional floods loosening the new structure. Work was not restarted until April 1622 and the bridge was not ready for use until 1624; indeed work continued on it until 1634. The total cost in materials and fees was approximately £13,500.

The width of the bridge varies from 17 to 19 feet and it has refuges above the cutwater-piers for the protection of pedestrians. Fifteen arches of varying span from 24 to 75 feet carry it a total length of 1164 feet; the fourteenth arch from Tweedmouth side rises to 45 feet, providing headroom for sailing vessels at the deepest part of the river. This gave rise to the old saw: 'The middle arch of Berwick Bridge is at one end'. Another rhyme noted:

> I am a Brigg as Travellers weel do ken,
> For English, Scottish and all other men.

There is no proof of the nineteenth-century assertion that this was carved on the bridge. The sixth pier from Berwick has the largest refuges and the highest parapet and, writing in 1799, Dr Fuller said: 'The sixth pillar separates Berwick from the county Palatine of Durham. The battlements at the outlets at this pillar are always covered with sods as a guide to constables and others in the execution of warrants for the apprehension of delinquents'. He continued: 'The south gate of the town, together with the adjoining guardhouse, shut up the bridge at its northerly extremity. Towards the middle of it there are two strong wooden barriers 148 feet distant from each other. In order to give additional security to this mode of defence, they

The new church of Holy Trinity, Berwick, built 1650-51 by the London mason John Young, using stone from Berwick Castle, was first used in June 1652. It was the only church to be built in England during the Commonwealth, and in its design and construction it was unyieldingly puritan (*Neil Potts*).

are made to project considerably beyond the battlements'. Fuller is referring to the defensive gateway that was designed by the military engineer Dugall Campbell to replace the medieval Bridge (English) Gate in 1743. Bridge Gate was removed in 1825. The Old Bridge carried the Great North Road up to 1928.

George Home, the great supporter of the bridge project, exerted considerable influence over Berwick. He was a prominent courtier and High Treasurer of Scotland and had attended the king at Berwick in 1603. He was granted all the lands in Berwick not belonging to the freemen. His actions on law and order greatly reduced Border crime and the severity of his measures, at Jedburgh in particular, gave rise to the phrase 'Jeddart justice'. His death was a great loss to the town and court.

James VI & I died on 27 March 1625, having only visited Berwick (and Scotland) once more in 1617, even though he had promised both Berwicker and Scot alike that he would visit them often; he was in Berwick from 10-13 May on his way to Scotland and again on 7 August when he returned to England. James was succeeded by his son Charles who had been born at Dunfermline in 1600. There is very little contemporary material concerning Carolean Berwick, but the Berwick public library holds an anonymous manuscript (*British Library MS Harley 7017,ff 167-168*) description of the town early in the reign of Charles I. The manuscript tells of the administration and garrisoning of the town and mentions 'certaine old Men named the foot Garrison who were allowed pay for picking the Walls and keeping them cleane'. The pre-seventeenth century ramparts are also described and the 'skoot nightly of shott & Pikemen that lay without the Walls to give warneing if any enimie approachd by shooting of a small piece. Then was there a Cannon called the Alarum Gun discharged within the Towne and the common Bell rung out....' The defence of the town was of particular interest to the writer, who emphasises the night security which included 'certaine Pentioners....who had the watch word....' The punishment for a man sleeping on duty 'was to hang over the Wall in a Baskett and there to stay for certain hourse, with bread & Water for his food & a penknife to cut the rope after the time of his punishment was expired, and so he fell into a Stanke without dainger of Drowneing'. Those who were 'litigious or quarrelsome' in the night were placed astride a cannon while it was fired.

The manuscript describes the 'fairest wind Mills' in the town, the bridge, the pier, the salmon fishing and the dilapidated castle with remains of 'faire Houses' and sculpture. The palace is also mentioned, with its commodious staff and storage areas, but it is noted that by this date it was 'almost levell with the ground, the goodly houses gone to decay, obsolete and worne out'. Very 'decent to behold' was the 'churching' of the mayor and corporation and the riding of the bounds. Pensioners in the town did guard duty, but also 'noe other service than to pray for the preservation of his Royall Majestie & his Progenie'.

On 2 June 1633 Charles I arrived in Berwick on his way to Scotland to be crowned; he was met at Berwick bridge by the mayor and commonalty and was addressed by the recorder, Sir Thomas Widdrington. With the king were a number of men who were to achieve immortality in the pages of history, men like William Laud, Archbishop of Canterbury, one of Charles's foremost advisers, and Sir Edward Coke the the legal expert. Charles dated letters from 'His Majesty's Palace in Berwick' and left the town for Scotland on 12 June, to be met at the Bound Road by the Scottish nobility. He returned to Berwick from Edinburgh on 16 July and after his return to London he ordered that most of the remaining Berwick ordnance be sent to London. The pieces from Berwick's walls were shipped aboard the *Gift of God* from Berwick quay by December 1633.

Although the two kingdoms had one monarch, the individual interests and aspirations of England and Scotland were not so united. Non-parliamentary government lasted from 1629 until 1640 and Charles I attempted to impose uniformity of church discipline on a reluctant Scotland; this was to lead to rebellion. Close to the Scottish Lowlands, the folk of Berwick were able to monitor the position, for Calvinism was strong amongst their immediate neighbours.

The Scots were alarmed at Charles's marriage to the Catholic Henrietta Maria and the efforts to maintain episcopacy. The Scots middle class who had given so much support to John Knox were particularly unhappy, but Charles, supported by William Laud, was determined to force bishops on the reluctant Scots. The issue of a new prayer book in Scotland in 1637 was the last straw and the Scots drew up their own National Covenant which rejected the recent religious changes. Although the Covenanters swore loyalty to Charles as king, they formally adopted Presbyterianism as the national religion, which precipitated the first of the Bishops' Wars in 1639. Determined to be obeyed, Charles moved the incompetent northern trained bands to the Border. On the advice of Sir Jacob Astley, Charles I's agent in Scotland, Berwick was occupied by the Earl of Essex. On 28 May 1639, Charles arrived at Berwick and lodged in the town until his tent was ready at the Birks of Berwick (later known as Yarrow Haugh); some two miles west between West Ord and Horncliff, this area was to become very popular with Victorian picnickers who held 'kettles', an alfresco meal taking its name from the fish-kettle used in cooking salmon fresh from the river).

The Journal of John Aston, 'privy chamber-man in extraordinary' to the king, who attended him in Berwick, noted how the condition of seventeenth-century Berwick's buildings was 'very meane'. Aston speaks of the troop movements in Berwick in 1639; the Earl of Lindsay was here with a garrison of 2500 and the Earl of Newcastle was quartered in the town with 200 cavalry who regularly patrolled the Border. The streets of the town were clogged with human and animal filth, and the king's servant, Edward Norgate, recorded: 'There is scarcity of provisions in Berwick, soldiers snatching people's dinners from them'.

The Scottish army were well-disciplined, owing to the presence of veterans from the Thirty Years' War, and were well supplied with arms and with leaders like Alexander Leslie, who had been a Field-Marshal in the Swedish army. On 7 June 1639 articles of pacification were signed at Berwick between Charles and the Scots by which treaty the two sides agreed to disband their armies, and restore the royal castles to Charles who conceded that a Parliament should decide civil matters and an Assembly ecclesiastical matters in Scotland. When Charles left Berwick on 28 July, Sir Marmaduke Ernle was left in command of the town, and the fortifications were refurbished and the gates strengthened.

Charles, however, persisted in his determination to maintain episcopacy. Asserting the Presbyterian religion, the Scots claimed a veto on the appointment of governors to Scottish castles and a second Bishops' War was precipitated in 1640. The Scots easily defeated the English army at Newburn-on-Tyne and seized Newcastle.

In August 1642 the Civil War broke out in England and the Scots were largely observers until in 1643 they agreed to help the parliamentary side. Berwick was garrisoned by the Scots while the Scottish army was in England up to 1647, and held out against attack by the Earl of Newcastle. On 28 April 1648 it was taken by the royalists Sir Marmaduke Langdale and Sir Charles Lucas with a company of 120 horse. They were ousted by 15 September 1648 and Cromwell appeared in the vicinity. Cromwell placed a regiment of foot at Berwick and used the town as a base for provisions for his army; in fact he billeted his soldiers 'free' on the burgesses. On 21 September 1648 Cromwell took up quarters at Mordington House and on 30 September he entered the town. Charles I was executed at Whitehall on 30 January 1649 and Great Britain became a Protectorate under Oliver Cromwell, during which time Berwick remained a frontier garrison town of great importance and improvements to the fortifications were carried out. While this was going on a second great seventeenth-century structure was being erected at Berwick.

Holy Trinity Church, Wallace Green ('the green by the walls'), abutting the Parade which was established as an open space with its own character by 1610, was built 1648-50 on the initiative of the Governor of Berwick, the Roundhead Colonel George Fenwicke of Brinkburne House (d.1656). The church is set close to the site of the medieval church of the same name (see page 38), and within its graveyard, and it was built by the mason John Young of Blackfriars, London. Its design has been called 'uncompromisingly Puritan', but as Nicklaus Pevsner pointed out, it is in the 'London style'. The church has been compared in style with St Katharine Cree within the City of London which was built during 1628-30. The rectangular building has no tower, which tradition would have us believe was at the request of Oliver Cromwell. There is, incidentally, no truth in the old local story that Cromwell and his men stabled their horses in the church. The exterior is very much as it was originally, but the west front is flanked by nineteenth-century polygonal towers. In the middle of the west front is a doorway with pediment on Tuscan columns, and Venetian windows above and to the sides. The chancel and vestry of the church were added in 1855; the former replacing a large Gothic window. The battlements finish off the aisle and facing south is a sundial with flanking scrolls.

Inside, the rectangular nave has two aisles but no chancel. With its arcade of five bays on Tuscan columns, and Venetian windows, the church is of distinctive character; while the north, south and east galleries have disappeared, the west gallery maintains the Jacobean style. The reredos (the structure behind the altar) is an early piece of work by Sir Edward Lutyens with Tuscan columns and balustrade against the east window. The pulpit is of around 1652. The west window was donated in 1855 by D.C. Marjoribanks MP, incorporates the seal of the old borough and includes some fine seventeenth-century Flemish medallions which were formerly in the private chapel of the Duke of Buckingham at Canons Park, Middlesex. The clere-story (upper storey of the nave walls) was given Venetian windows in 1855. In recent years a new high altar has been set up, and in 1980 a parish room was created by screening off the former Lady Chapel on the north side of the church. The masonry of the church was completed by 11 November 1651 and stone from the castle was used. The new church was used for the first time in June 1652 and the medieval church (set just to the south) was rapidly demolished. The building was not consecrated until 1662.

The monuments inside are of great interest and commemorate Berwick's chief citizens since the seventeenth century. In particular there is the monument of 1656 to Col. Fenwicke himself, and one to Dr George Johnston (1797-1858), the 'founder, the life and soul' of the Berwickshire Naturalists' Club (1831). Here too is another Berwick link with St Andrews, for the minister and diarist James Melville (1556-1614), nephew of the celebrated Andrew Melville, founding father of Scottish Presbyterianism, is commemorated by a memorial of 1919. He was an exile and died in Berwick. For his second wife, Melville married the daughter of Richard Clerke, Vicar of Berwick. The town's vicars too have made their mark, not least the Rev. John Smithson, Vicar from 1664, who was hanged at Berwick in 1672 for the murder of his wife.

In Scotland they now prepared to welcome the new king Charles II. Although he found the new Covenanting religion

The Castle and the Tweed by Joseph Mallord William Turner (1775-1851), clearly showing the Bell Tower, the Mill at Tommy the Miller's Fields, the Town Hall, the now vanished windmill, and the White Wall leading down to the riverside gun tower. The 15-arched Old Bridge spans the Tweed to the right and the salmon fishers ply their trade in the foreground. Turner prepared the original of this engraving in his Berwick sketchbook during his visit to Sir Walter Scott's home at Abbotsford in 1831. It was ultimately engraved by W. Miller in 1833 for Scott's *Poetical Works*.

distasteful, Charles decided to sign an agreement accepting its dogmas and sailed out of exile in Europe. He entered the Spey on 23 June 1650. Inevitably the parliamentarian army mobilised and under Oliver Cromwell marched from the south of England. On 13 July Cromwell was again in Berwick where he was received 'graciously' by the mayor and commonalty and once more set up his headquarters at Mordington House.

The Scots leader General David Leslie was defeated at Dunbar by Cromwell on 3 September. By September of the following year the Governor's House at Berwick was handed over to the Commonwealth. Cromwell was now master of the land south of the Forth, but on New Year's Day 1651, Charles II was crowned king at Scone. As Cromwell's army advanced towards

Perth, Charles decided on a sally into England. Cromwell turned his army around and, pursuing Charles, caught up with the royalists at Worcester; here he routed them completely on 3 September 1651, and Charles fled to Normandy. For nine years Berwick folk observed the authoritarian English Puritan regime in Scotland, backed up with military force. On 17 August 1657 Cromwell was proclaimed Chief Magistrate of the United Kingdom at Berwick, after which there was much civic feasting. In 1660 General George Monk marched south with a regiment that would become the Coldstream Guards to negotiate the return of Charles II. By this time Oliver Cromwell was dead (1658) and the Protectorate of his son Richard had been short-lived. In 1659 a terrible fire raged in Berwick in which much property was destroyed; the Berwick royalists saw it as a cleansing of the Puritan regime on the eve of a new reign.

On 25 May 1660 Charles II landed at Dover; at Berwick Scot and Englishman jostled to drink the health in free wine of the Covenanting king. But episcopacy returned with the new king and religious strife boiled up again. In 1684 Berwick's charter was surrendered to English royalists; a new one was drawn up but never signed. The old charter was to be restored by King William in 1689.

Charles II died at Whitehall in February 1685 and was succeeded by his Roman Catholic brother as James VII & II. In a matter of months there were rebellions on both sides of the Border with the object of putting the Duke of Monmouth (Charles II's bastard by Lucy Walters) on the throne. In Scotland Monmouth's supporters were guillotined on 29 June 1685 and Monmouth himself was defeated at Sedgemoor on 15 July. The 'Killing Time' now got into full swing as the royalist John Graham of Claverhouse, 'Bonnie Dundee', swept through the south-west Borders in pursuit of the Covenanters. Although neither Covenanter nor papist believed in toleration, King James's Declarations and Letters of Indulgence (1686-88) gave freedom of worship, but there were many who saw the restoration of Roman Catholicism as nigh. The birth of a son to James and his second wife, the Catholic Mary of Modena, on 10 June

A rare woodcut of early-Victorian Berwick from the west by a Northumbrian artist for M.A. Richardson's *The Borderer's Table Book*. It shows Berwick *circa* 1845, and pinpoints the extant windmills of the burgh and the Town Hall. Tweedmouth and Spittal lie on the south shore of the Tweed and are clearly separated by moorland at this date.

1688 precipitated action and they opened negotiations with James's Protestant nephew William of Orange to replace James on the throne. William landed at Torbay in November 1688 and James VII & II fled. On 16 December 1688 the commander of the Berwick garrison, Lt.Col. Rupert Billingsley, informed the mayor and commonalty that he and his men would support William; the mayor and commonalty wisely concurred.

On 20 February 1702, while riding at Hampton Court, King William was thrown from his horse; he broke his collar bone and pleurisy followed to accelerate his death on 8 March. Berwick sent its condolences to his sister-in-law—Mary having died in 1694—and prepared for the new century.

The sixteenth and seventeenth centuries saw Berwick's only associations with witchcraft. There were few cases of prosecutable witchcraft in the south-east Borders, and Berwick had no great 'celebrity cases' like that of John Fian and the North Berwick witches. Since the fifteenth century Berwick had been subject to English law, so the Acts against witchcraft of 1542, 1562 and 1601 applied in the borough. An Act of 1736 penalised those who 'pretended to use witchcraft etc'. The Vagrancy Act of 1824 was amended in 1950 to cover cases of reputed witchcraft. The main references to witchcraft in Berwick are fourfold:

1. In a letter from Henry, Lord Hunsdon, to Sir Henry Widdrington, dated 6 March 1590, there is this note: That King James VI & I of Scotland was requesting that a 'witch' dwelling in Berwick be surrendered to him. Apparently she had taken refuge in Berwick from the Scottish witchhunters. Scotland was still enacting the Witchcraft Act of 1563, and in 1604 the Act *Anentis Witchcraft* was brought into force north of the Border.

2. During the governorship of Peregrine, Lord Willoughby, another witch is recorded in the Berwick *Council Book* of 1598: 'We find and present that, by the information and oath of credible witnesses Richard Swynbourne's wife hath of long time dealt with three several women witches for the bewitching of one William, garrison man, who did answer that they would not hurt him, but that a man witch must do it; which the said Swynbourne's wife hath confessed to this presently....'

3. This case is quoted by John Sykes in his *Historical Register of Remarkable Events*: (30 July 1649) 'At a private guild holden at Berwick, before the Rt. Worshipful Andrew Crispe Esq, Mayor, Mr Stephen Jackson, alderman, and the rest of the guild brethren, it was ordered according to the guild's desire, that a man which tryeth the witches in Scotland shall be sent for, and satisfaction to be given him by the towne in defraying his charges, and in coming hither, and that the towne shall engage that no violence be offered him by any persons within the towne'.

4. In 1673 a certain Ann Armstrong of Birchen Nooke deposed that 'on the second day of May laste, at nighte, the witches carried her to Berwick bridge end, where she saw a great

Berwick's 'Old Bridge' is the fifth known bridge built across the Tweed on or near this site. Work was carried out on the bridge during 1611-24 but the construction was not completed until 1634. At a total length of 1164 ft, the bridge has fifteen arches of which the sixth pier from the Berwick side formerly marked the boundary between the burgh and the county of North Durham (*Neil Potts*).

number of them'. (See: Surtees Society, Vol XL. *Depositions from the Castle of York*, 1861.)

Under the date 1 August 1629 in the *Register of the Privy Council* (2nd series, v.3, p.270) is this: 'Commission to the sheriff of Berwick and his deputies to try Helen Huldie in Coldinghame for witchcraft'. The same *Register* (p.270) also records, 'Commission to the sheriff of Berwick and his deputies for the trial of Sara Meslet and Easter Moreis in Foulden, and Isabel Cunninghame in Paxtane called "Blewsleaves" for witchcraft'. But there is no evidence that anyone was ever executed for witchcraft in Berwick.

CHAPTER 9

Georgian and Regency Berwick

An impression of Berwick in the eighteenth century can be got from Dr. John Fuller's *History*. All the main streets known today within the walls were extant, but two were known by different names. Back Way was to become Ravensdowne and Shaw's Lane became Chapel Street. Between Shaw's Lane and High Street were cultivated gardens with a common way from approximately where the Victorian public library was in Marygate to the junction of modern Church Street and Chapel Street. There were three large expanses of rough land between the modern police station (1900) site and Ravensdowne. Fuller comments that the buildings 'generally are of freestone covered with red tiles', the houses for the most part being of three stories and 'highly commodious'. There was a good shopping area, he says, with shops exhibiting 'an appearance of neatness and elegancy'. The streets remained irregular and 'intolerably ill-paved', but 'wide and commodious'. Several households had paid for pavements outside their own premises. There was little street lighting and at night a few 'glimmering lamps' whose faint light 'assists [the pedestrians] but little in avoiding nuisances'. There was some 'subscription lighting' in High Street and Hide Hill.

A walk down modern Ravensdowne offers some good examples of eighteenth-century urban building. The street began in the thirteenth century as Ravensden ('the dene of the ravens'), then was known in the fifteenth century as Finkel Street ('the street with the bend in it'), and Ratten Row ('the rat infested street') in the sixteenth century. Back Way was its name to Fuller's contemporaries, and at the top of Ravensdowne is the former military hospital of *circa* 1745; it replaced an earlier and smaller infirmary on the same site. At No. 30 Ravensdowne stands the renovated pair of cottages of the 1790s associated with the two adjoining ice-houses (see page 149). Numbers

Berwick from Tweedmouth shore in 1745, at the time when the fortifications were being improved following the alarm caused by the Jacobite rebellion of 1745-46. The gateway designed by the military engineer Dugall Campbell, seen at the Berwick end of the Old Bridge, and known as Bridge Gate or English Gate, had replaced a seventeenth-century entrance in 1743. Bridge Gate was removed in 1825. The preposterously out-of-proportion print was drawn by N. Buck and engraved by W.H. Lizars and appeared in Frederick Sheldon's *History of Berwick-upon-Tweed* of 1849.

8,16,20 and 26 Ravensdowne date after 1783. Nearby Ness Street (sixteenth-century Leadenhall Street) also has some fine but plain eighteenth-century houses. Avenue House, in Palace Street East, with its colourful coat of arms of the Call family, is a fine Georgian dwelling opposite to which is The Avenue containing The Retreat, the red brick house of 1740 which was built perhaps as a home for a retired soldier. Hide Hill also has some good eighteenth-century properties. Numbers 34-36 (Popinjay's Restaurant) were built in 1718-19 by Captain Thomas Philips, the engineer working on the construction of Berwick Barracks; the dwelling's arched stable area at the rear can still be seen. Dewar's Lane (off Bridge Street) contains large eighteenth-century town granaries.

The eighteenth century was seen in by the accession in 1702 of James VII & II's daughter Anne in succession to her brother-in-law William III who had reigned conjointly from 1689 to 1694 with her sister Mary, and thereafter on his own. With the merging of the parliaments of Scotland and England by the Act of Union , made law at Westminster on 1 May 1707, Berwick's normal trading activities with Scotland were resumed, and by 1750 the town had become a flourishing port once more. By 1799 a few weavers were still producing linen in their own homes, and William Scott set up a damask factory in Castlegate in 1784. Sacking too was established by Thomas Cockburn in the Greenses in 1793, and Dr Fuller tells us: 'The men earn from 6s (30p) to 15s (75p) weekly, women from 2s 6d (12½p) to 4s (20p) and children from 1s (5p) to 2s 6d'. Cockburn was something of a diverse entrepreneur, for by 1795 he was manufacturing felts for paper mills, flannels, broadcloths and waggon covers, and at the New Water Haugh 'factory' he manufactured snuff, a venture he had begun in 1778. James Clunie & Co. owned a prosperous sailcloth factory established in 1793, and their spinners worked on flax and hemp imported from St Petersburg and Riga, their biggest markets being on the Thames and the Tyne. During the Napoleonic Wars Berwick sailcloth was extensively used by the Royal Navy. Clunie & Co. it was who set up Berwick's bleachfields at Spring Gardens in 1793. From 1788 to 1792 a Mr McCay established a cotton and muslin factory in Berwick while Edward Grey, Archibald Inglis and Roger Struther each manufactured worsted and thread stockings. In Castlegate there was a carpet factory belonging to William Graham who first set up his looms around 1778. Hatmaking was established at Berwick by Mr Hubback, whose men at 21/- (£1.05) to 25/- (£1.25) a week were amongst the highest paid in the town, while Mr Porteous was a prominent Castlegate dyer of silk, cotton and stuff from 1795. The currying of leather was established in Berwick in 1784 by John Morrison, while shoes and boots were made by George and William Thompkins; shoes made from wooden heels and soles (clogs) were manufactured by both Thomson and Scott of Tweedmouth. A tannery was established by Knowles, Marshall & Co. in Berwick about this time too, and they owned one of the few horse mills for grinding the bark used in the tanning process. There was also some glovemaking in eighteenth-century Berwick.

The gateway to Berwick Barracks at the Parade, built in 1719. The Barracks were completed in 1721 under the direction of Captain Thomas Philips and the architect to the Office of Ordnance, Andrew Jeffe. The gateway displays the arms of George I, which are quartered for England and Scotland, France, Ireland and Hanover and sport the white horse of Hanover (see page 199) *(Neil Potts)*.

In 1799 Berwick had two shipping companies, the Old Shipping Co., established in 1764, and the Union Shipping Co.

of 1794. Twenty-one smacks operated out of the quay to London, Edinburgh and Glasgow. The shipping trade brought spinoffs for Berwick.

Ships were built both in Berwick and Tweedmouth at three shipyards: Gowans of Berwick, and the Bruce and Joseph Todd & Co. yards at Tweedmouth. In Berwick sails were manufactured by John Miller Dickson, a partner in the Berwick Roperie Co., established in 1794. There were several roperies in Berwick at this time supplying the shipbuilders, the chandlers and the fishing vessel owners and the netmakers. Whilst there was no iron-making in Berwick, two naileries supplied such trades as the carpenters and housebuilders, and the most prominent nailer was Mrs Wilson of Bridge Street.

Fuller tells us that from 1761 until about 1770 the walls of Berwick were almost completely rebuilt in many parts; these sections are known as the Georgian Walls today. After the alarm raised by the Jacobite rising of 1745-46 the Elizabethan Walls, the medieval walls and the seventeenth-century embankments were repaired and a bomb-proof well-buttressed garrison magazine was built behind high walls in 1749 near Windmill Mount. The wall from Ness Gate (inserted during 1815-16 to give access to the new pier) to the New Road is an eighteenth-century construction set on the medieval walls and includes Fisher's Fort and Coxon's Tower. Fisher's is a six-gunport artillery battery of around the late 1750s; the Russian cannon displayed here was captured in the Crimean War of 1854-56; the other guns once mounted here were requisitioned for scrap in World War II. The four-gun battery flanks the look-out tower, called Coxon's Tower, and leads round to the thirteen-gun Saluting Battery (in front of Wellington Terrace). The Eight Gun Battery (it actually has nine gun emplacements) was built around 1744 and defends the entrance to the river. From here the walls are known as the Quay Walls and had houses built up against the back of the fortifications. The Stonegate, formerly known as Fish Port (or Fish Gate) was rebuilt in the 1760s and still retains its wooden doors. The defences fronting the old quay were completed by 1765. The knowledge that Berwick's

Berwick's Town Hall dominates the view as the visitor emerges from Castlegate through the Scotsgate and into Marygate, the burgh's high street. To the right the old AI slices through what was Golden Square, once a spacious yard, which was breached to make the road leading to the New Bridge of 1928. To the left is Walkergate, once the street of fullers, or cloth dressers (*Neil Potts*).

defences were so strong caused the Jacobite armies to avoid the town.

Berwick was largely a spectator during the Jacobite rebellions, although Roman Catholic landowners like James Radcliffe, 3rd Earl of Derwentwater, joined in proclaiming James Francis Edward Stuart as the true king at Morpeth, Alnwick and Kelso. When George I succeeded Anne on 1 August 1714, the mayor and commonalty at Berwick joined with the Duke of Roxburgh to send their loyal greetings, and each member of the Guild received 2/- (10p) to toast the new king. On hearing that Derwentwater and Thomas Forster, MP for Northumberland, had risen in favour of the Pretender, the town formed ten companies of forty men each in its defence; the companies were disbanded in 1716. To assist with the range of the guns on the walls eleven houses were demolished in the Greenses and Castlegate, but Berwick was never attacked;

compensation for the loss of the dwellings was not paid until 1720.

Local Jacobite sympathisers were jailed at the Town Hall, including a curious couple, the uncle and nephew Launcelot and Mark Errington. The antiquary Francis Grose first gave literary prominence, with much exaggeration, to the story of how the Erringtons had tricked the small garrison at Holy Island castle and had displayed the Pretender's banner on the battlements. The king's troops from Berwick quickly arrested the pair but ultimately the Erringtons were sprung from jail at Berwick and escaped.

Several companies of Dutch and Hessian troops had passed through Berwick on their way to join the Hanoverian commander Sir John Cope's army at Dunbar. In the first great trial of arms between the government troops and the Jacobites, Cope was defeated at Gladsmuir (Prestonpans) on 20 September 1745; he fled to Berwick via Coldstream and was in Berwick by 22 September. The town was also to play host to the routed troops of Hamilton's, Gardiner's, and Whitney's regiments which had served with Sir John. Cope has been unfairly maligned as incompetent by such as Robert Burns who re-worked a Jacobite ballad for the *Scots Musical Museum* telling of Cope's supposed inefficiency and his flight. The ballad 'Hey Johnie Cope, are ye wauken yet?' was probably written by Adam Skirving (1719-1803), a Haddington farmer. In Burns's version the Berwick references are:

> Sir Johnie into Berwick rade,
> Just as the devil had been his guide;
> Gien him the warld he would na stay'd
> To foughten the boys in the morning.
>
> Says the Berwickers unto Sir John,
> O what's become of all your men,
> In faith, says he, I dinna ken,
> I left them a' this morning.

After Cope's defeat, Berwick was put on military alert and the townsfolk kept note of Charles Edward's Stuart's march to

The time-worn columns of the frontage of the Main Guard look out onto the renovated houses at Palace Street. The eighteenth-century Main Guard guardhouse was removed to its present site from Marygate in 1815 when it was no longer needed by the army. It is believed to be the earliest piece of preservation work in Berwick (*Neil Potts*).

Derby and subsequent retreat. Shadowing the Jacobite army, and travelling up the east coast, Hanoverian troops passed through Berwick led by Major-General Henry Hawley and Major-General John Huske. As Frederick Sheldon says: 'The burghers of Berwick, in imitation of the gentry and inhabitants of the Merse [Berwickshire] and Lothians, furnished horses to transport the baggage and provisions for the men; each soldier got bread and beef, and a glass of whiskey [*sic*]; the bells were rung in honour of their arrival, and the loyal inhabitants of Berwick testified their joy by an illumination on a small scale, the windows of the Jacobites being smashed to pieces by the loyal mob'.

Hawley was defeated at Falkirk and the government now sent HRH William Augustus, Duke of Cumberland, the second son of George II, to destroy the Jacobites once and for all.

Cumberland passed through Berwick on his way north on 30 January 1746 and defeated Charles Edward Stuart and his ill-fed and ill-equipped army at Culloden Moor on 16 April. On 12 August 1771 Cumberland was to be in Berwick again and was met at the bridge by the mayor, John Balderstone, who escorted him to the Governor's House. There he was wined and dined by the corporation who presented him with the Freedom of the Town in a gold box. A ball was held in his honour at the Assembly Rooms at the Town Hall and His Royal Highness had time to survey and be told about all the great building projects that had taken place in the previous sixty years.

From the 1660s or so there had been frequent complaints by Berwick folk about the billeting of soldiers in public and private houses in the town. In 1705 the mayor wrote to the town's two MPs and to the governor of the garrison asking them to use their influence to have a barracks built at Berwick. In 1709 a site was chosen at the top of Church Street (the old Soutergate, the street of the shoemakers), where the old Parade School (1856) was later sited near to the former Tudor stables. Plans were delayed until 1717 when the present site of the barracks alongside the seventeenth-century Parade was decided upon. The engineer in charge of the building was Captain Thomas Philips, and Andrew Jeffe, architect to the Office of Ordnance, worked on the gateway (1719). Materials came from all parts of the borough: stone from the castle, rubble and infill from houses demolished in Castlegate and the Greenses in 1715, and bricks made from Tweedmouth Moor clay. The building was completed in May 1721, and in July the soldiers moved in; their furniture and utensils had been supplied by the townspeople, anxious to speed the soldiers' taking up residence. Above the gateway of the barracks are displayed the distinctive arms of George I. The arms contain the four quarters for Scotland and England, for France, for Ireland and for Hanover. The barracks are set around a square of three-storey blocks. The first bay of each four-bay building was for officers, and the other bays were for soldiers who lived eight to a room. A garrison of 600 men and 36 officers could be housed.

'His Majesty's Good Town of Berwick-on-Tweed' seen from the Tweed's south shore at Carr Rock. This plate (and the six that follow) were engraved by Robert Scott (1771-1841), the Lanark-born engraver, from the drawings of Alexander Carse (fl.1812-20). They were the first published views of Berwick and appeared in Dr John Fuller's *The History of Berwick upon Tweed* (1799). Scott was considered the best Scottish engraver of his time and first won recognition for his set of 'Edinburgh Views' of 1795-96. Carse was celebrated for his scenes of Scottish domestic life, often containing humorous features.

At the junction of Palace Street and Palace Green stands the eighteenth-century Main Guard. It was once set in Marygate (where the bus station is now) and was moved to this location in 1815 when its function as a guardhouse ended. The building contains two rooms to accommodate officers and men and a 'black-hole' lock-up. Its re-siting is probably the earliest example in Berwick of the preservation of an historic building.

Set on the east side of Palace Green is the Governor's House, built around 1719 as the dwelling of the military governors of Berwick. By the eighteenth century the post of Governor of Berwick—which was abolished in 1833—was a sinecure usually given to a general nearing retirement age. Since 1833 the house has been variously a residence for officers at the

garrison and a motor repair works. It is now owned by the
Lindisfarne Liqueur Co. who have their Wine Museum at the
rear (see page 205). Palace Green, incidentally, is worthy of note,
for here in medieval times was the administrative quarters of
central government. It contained the garrison's victualling
offices, storehouses, a bakery and a brewhouse.

Berwick's Town Hall, set at the foot of Marygate, dominates
the town from all angles. It is the successor to a number of
medieval tolbooths and town halls within the same area which
was a focus for the weekly markets from the early Middle Ages.
By the 1740s the immediate precursor of the present Town
Hall, a sixteenth-century building with spire and clock, set on
stone arches, had fallen into disrepair, so the burgesses
urgently set in motion a plan for its replacement. Samuel and
John Worral of London were paid £31-10s-0d to supply plans,
elevations and sections for a new building. However, the
borough Guild rejected their ideas and contracted with a fellow
guildsman, Joseph Dods, to act as architect; Dods's name is
recorded above the entrance. The style of the Town Hall is that
of James Gibb's St Martin's-in-the-Fields in London. The
building was begun in 1750 and the whole was completed in
1761; by 1754 the west front, cells, spire and first-floor rooms
were completed, and after that date the Town Hall was
extended to the east, obviously as an afterthought. A high flight
of steps leads up to the Tuscan columns of the front elevation.
The ground floor contained a cell area which was restored in the
1970s and is now used as a coffee house and gift shop. The east
ground floor was the Exchange where markets were held for the
sale of dairy products, meat and poultry, and the use of this
market area has been resumed. The first floor of the Town Hall
was used for guild meetings, local and political elections and for
the borough quarter sessions which were discontinued in 1951.
Within the council chamber is a figure of Justice,
commissioned from the local artist Joseph Alexander in 1789
for £5. The mayor's parlour contains the town's ceremonial
halberds which have the initials of Ferdinando Forster, mayor
of Berwick from 1685-86. The upper floor of the Town Hall

Berwick Barracks were the first purpose-built barracks in the British Isles, and work started on them in 1717. The two main blocks abutting the square to left and right cost £6000, and the garrison moved in in 1721. The 'Clock Block', facing, was not constructed until *circa* 1746. The Barracks was the Depot of the King's Own Scottish Borderers from 1881 to 1964; the Regimental Museum is still housed in 'O' Block, formerly the officers' quarters.

housed the debtors' and felons' jails, and it seems that break-outs were quite common in the eighteenth century.

The bellchamber of the Town Hall contains eight bells which were recast in 1754, and a curfew bell still tolls each evening (except Sunday) at eight o'clock. It is interesting to note that although still used for civic functions, the Town Hall does not belong to the town. It was built wholly by the Guild and is still a part of the Freemen's Estate run by the Berwick-upon-Tweed Corporation (Freemen) Trustees, and this body has recently restored the building with the help of the Historic Buildings Council.

An essential part of the eighteenth-century gentleman's equipage was his carriage, and the period also saw the development of the posting business in Berwick. Because of the steepness of West Street and Eastern Lane, the coaches which clattered through Berwick made a horseshoe route through the Scotsgate, down Marygate and Hide Hill into Bridge Street and across the Old Bridge. The well-heeled eighteenth-century traveller had the option of travelling in his own carriage, drawn by his own horses, or travelling post with hired horses from stage to stage, or hiring a postchaise and horses. Four kinds of carriage were commonly seen on Berwick's streets in the eighteenth century: the sociable, which was a low-hung angular carriage with two seats facing each other of which the rear seat could be covered with a folding hood; the barouche-landau which was a stately carriage hung high on cee springs with a double folding head which enabled it to be completely enclosed if desired; the post-chariot which was a small closed carriage made to seat two, some having seats at the 'rumble' for two servants; and the postchaise which was technically a chariot, drawn by one pair of horses—usually the postchaises were painted yellow. Unlike private carriages, the postchaises travelled at a gallop and consequently the life of a post-horse was short. The cost of hiring a pair of post-horses in Berwick varied from 1s. (5p) to 1s.6d. (7½p) with the same for a postboy to drive; the cost of the postchaise worked out at around 3d (1p) per mile. Although there were to be many regular public carriages on the Great North Road through Berwick by 1800, in the 1760s the thought of sharing a public vehicle was abhorrent to the gentry, so the Berwick inns did a roaring trade in carriage hire and several of Berwick's coaching inns were famous on the London to Edinburgh run. The Red Lion, Marygate, on the site where Woolworths is now, was an important eighteenth and nineteenth-century coaching inn, as was the King's Arms Hotel in Hide Hill. By 1791 a seventeenth-century tenement in Sandgate was converted into the inn called the Hen and Chickens which was used by the carriage trade and served also as a kind of club for the Northumberland Militia. The building had once been the home of William Selby (1705-77), the prominent apothecary and surgeon to the garrison who had his shop in Bridge Street.

One famous visitor to Berwick on Friday, 18 May 1787, was

The Governor's House, Palace Green, from the Quay Walls. This was the home of the former military governors of Berwick and was built in the early eighteenth century. The house now belongs to the Lindisfarne Liqueur Co who run a wine museum on the site. In the centre of the picture lies The Avenue, facing Avenue House. To the right the red-brick building of 1740 was probably a retired soldier's dwelling.

the poet Robert Burns. He wrote of his visit in his *Journal*: '...ride to Berwick—an idle town, but rudely picturesque—Meet Lord Errol in walking round the walls—his Lordship's flattering notice of me—dine with Mr Clunzie Merchant—nothing particular in company or conversation—' Of the people Burns met in Berwick, John Clunie was a freeman and magistrate and mayor during 1783-84; he was a partner in Clunie & Home, timber and iron merchants, Bridge Street. George, 16th Earl of Erroll (1767-98), was a soldier; having inadvertently disclosed a secret entrusted to him by William Pitt, he committed suicide; he had family connections in the area, his mother being the daughter of Sir William Carr of Etal. There is a tradition that Burns took a dislike to Berwick and its burgesses, although he stayed only a few hours, and according to J. Hardy in *The Denham Tracts* (1892), many believed the following piece of doggerel was composed by Burns:

> Berwick is a dirty place,
> Has a church without a steeple,
> A middenstead at every door
> And a damned deceitful people.

Hardy further quotes two alternative versions of the verse which were to become current in Berwick:

> 1802 version:
>
> Berwick is an ancient town
> A church without a steeple,
> A pretty girl at every door
> And very generous people.

> 1820 version:
>
> Berwick is a dirty town,
> A church without a steeple.
> There's a midden at every door,
> God curse all the people.

Burns does not mention in his *Journal* any visit to John Renton of Lamberton, of Mordington House. Renton sent Burns an invitation to ride and dine with him, and this note from the poet was found in Renton's papers:

> Your billet, sir, I grant receipt;
> Wi' you I'll canter ony gate,
> Though 'twere a trip to yon blue warl',
> Where birkies march on burning marl:
> Then, sir, God willing, I'll attend ye,
> And to His goodness I commend ye.

Incidentally, it seems that 'Burns Night' was first officially celebrated in Berwick on 25 January 1875.

Public entertainment in Berwick took a great step forward in the eighteenth century. From the reign of Edward IV, it is said, the 'Town Waits' entertained the mayor and corporation at civic functions like the mayor-making, public dinners and the Christmas Day procession to church, and their duties had developed out of the piping of the night watch. The Waits

The Elizabethan Walls at Wallace Green, with a clear view of Holy Trinity parish church and the Barracks. The pantiled roof of the house to the right represents a distinctive feature of Berwick. Until the eighteenth century most of Berwick's houses would be thatched, and this roofing was replaced by red pantiles and slates by Hanoverian times. Once the pantiles were made at such nearby places as Cocklaw; now they have to come from as far away as Hull.

entertained the Duke of Cumberland during his visit in 1771, and he must have been struck by their distinctive livery of blue cloak and cocked hat both faced with gold lace, as well as by the dreadfulness of their playing. The Waits were disbanded in 1808, and the last of them, the blind fiddler James Wallace of the Fiddle and Tam Inn, Shaw's Lane, lived until 1854. Itinerant musicians regularly came to Berwick in both the eighteenth and nineteenth centuries, but it was the development of the theatre that was to bring the town a higher standard of entertainment.

The Berwick Archives contain a note that travelling players were paid for entertaining in 1564, but in the two centuries that followed there was little or no theatrical activity in Berwick, probably due to the opposition of the local clergy. Dr Fuller mentions that 'theatrical performances have occasionally been exhibited in Berwick for a great number of years past, sometimes in the Town Hall, and sometimes in a house in Golden Square'. The latter may indeed refer to an old malthouse theatre used by 'Mr Fisher's Company' in 1770. Berwick's first permanent theatre was opened in 1794 by Stephen Kemble in disused premises at the rear of the King's Arms Hotel. The celebrated actor George Frederick Cooke (1756-1811), who had been brought up in Berwick and apprenticed to a printer in the town, played here in 1807. In 1808 the theatre was taken over by the father of William Charles Macready (1793-1873), the famous tragedian. The premises were burned down in 1845 and the King's Arms Assembly Rooms were built on the site. In the latter part of the nineteenth century drama and musical entertainments were staged at the Corn Exchange and the Queen's Rooms in Hide Hill.

By far the most time-consuming activity outside working hours for the eighteenth-century Berwick burgess was church attendance, and in the period 1719-1829 no fewer than eight churches were established. Church attendance was a mark of respectability and the church exerted a very strong discipline over its congregations. It was a place of public rebuke for moral misdemeanours of all kinds, and the Berwick clergy to a man frowned on playing cards, attending the theatre, drinking alcohol and travelling on a Sunday.

The first church to be established was the Low Meeting House, on the east side of Hide Hill (Hide Hill Street in the early nineteenth century) in today's Brown Bear public house yard. The church, built by public subscription in 1719, was a Presbyterian church, with origins as far back as John Knox's stay at Berwick during 1549-51; indeed it was often referred to as 'John Knox's Church'. Another public subscription church was the High Meeting House of 1724 on the north side of Hide Hill. The King's Own Scottish Borderers worshipped there after 1881 under their chaplain, the Rev. James Kean. St Andrew's Church, in Greenside Avenue (once reached by the old Cockle Steps, behind the Elizabethan Walls by the Scotsgate but now demolished), was formed as an

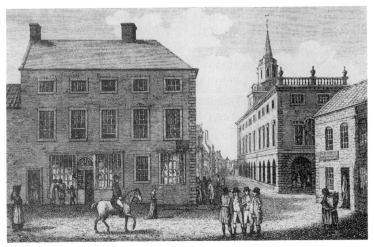

The Town Hall from Hide Hill looking up Marygate to the Scotsgate
— 'gate' being the English form of the old Norse *gata* meaning a street.
Apart from modern shop fronts this scene has changed very little,
although around 1400 the name Hide Hill superseded Uddingate.
The ground-floor area of the Town Hall has now been restored as a
coffee house and gift shop, and the balustrade around the roof has
long been removed.

amalgamation of the High and Low Meeting Houses: the
foundation stone was laid 16 July 1896 and it was opened for
worship on 2 May 1897.

The Burgher Meeting House was on the south side of the
High Street at Golden Square and was built in 1770 to be
enlarged in 1796. The congregation were strict Calvinists who
had withdrawn from the Church of Scotland in 1730. In those
days Golden Square, which incidentally has nothing
whatsoever to do with Berwick's medieval mint, was a yard
reached through an archway from Marygate (the whole was
demolished in 1927-28 to make way for a road leading to the
Royal Tweed Bridge). This church developed into the
congregation of Wallace Green Presbyterian Church, opened
for worship on 19 June 1859; this church with its 127ft steeple
was renovated in 1932. The Anti-Burgher Meeting House was
in Church Street in 1812, and this congregation objected to the

Burgher's Oath which supported Scotland's 'established religion', which they deemed to have fallen into error. The congregation founded St Aidan's Church in the old Dispensary Yard, and this closed in 1977 when they moved to Bankhill United Reformed Church. The latter was built as a Zion Chapel by seceders from the Anti-Burghers in 1835-36. In 1852 it was taken over by members of the Low Meeting House when that congregation was split by the Disruption of the Church of Scotland in 1843. Bankhill Church became part of the Presbyterian Church of England up to 1973 when it entered the United Reformed Church.

The Relief, or Middle, Meeting House of 1756 was situated at the east end of Shaw's Lane (Chapel Street), and this Presbyterian congregation insisted on choosing their own minister since they objected to the patronage system. In 1917 this church joined with the congregation in Church Street to form St Aidan's. Numbers 1-3 Walkergate ('the street of the cloth dressers') was the site of the Baptist Meeting House of 1810-11; the congregation moved to Castlegate in 1858 where they took over a church which had been established by an Independent Congregation in 1849. It was demolished in the mid-1980s to make way for a supermarket.

Berwick's Methodist Meeting House was built in 1797 in East Walkergate Lane. Methodism was greatly promoted in Berwick by the presence (on twenty occasions) of the movement's founder, John Wesley (1703-91), the English evangelist, who first came to the town on 20 July 1748. Wesley preached to a congregation estimated at 2000 on the bowling green (now under 2 Wellington Terrace) in Palace Green; there seems to have been 'a small society' of Methodists, probably owing to the work of one Robert Sutty, before Wesley's visit. On 1 June 1759 Wesley preached in the Town Hall, and thereafter he preached in this building on each of his visits. The Town Hall seems to have been used by the Methodists until 1797 (there were many 'dissenters' amongst the Guildsmen, who had sheltered non-conformist ministers during the years of persecution). Wesley was by no means complimentary to Berwick— 'this poor,

Built of New Mills and Edington stone during 1750-61, the Town Hall is the chief feature of this print of Marygate. On the left is the Main Guard, on the site of the modern bus station forecourt; and the Red Lion Inn sits on the site of modern Woolworths. The Red Lion was an important coaching inn right into the nineteenth century as Marygate formed part of the Great North Road as it passed through Berwick.

barren place' (May 1766); 'poor dead Berwick' (1768), he wrote in his *Journal*—but he was confident that Methodism would eventually flourish in the town. Wesley's visits led to the society's circuit preachers visiting also, and the burgesses heard such as Thomas Rankin and Christopher Hopper. Until 1783 Berwick's Methodists were in the 'Newcastle circuit', but it seems that many of their preachers worked out of Edinburgh; in 1783 Berwick's own circuit was formed with William Hunter as its first superintendent. The Methodist Church of 1878 was built on the site of the 1797 church. The Primitive Methodists— a revivalist body founded in 1812 and influential amongst the working class—formed a church, schoolroom and manse in College Place in 1829-30 and amalgamated with the Wesleyans in 1920 at the Walkergate Church. The door of the former manse displays a bust which is thought to be that of William Lister, superintendent of the Berwick circuit from 1833-36.

The Catholic Emancipation Act of 13 April 1829 led to the establishment of Roman Catholic worship in Berwick. Throughout the eighteenth century there had been only a handful of Catholics in Berwick served by chaplains from nearby Catholic homes, but in 1789 a group of French Catholic clergy sought refuge at Berwick following the French Revolution. Public Record Office Treasury Reports show that around 1796 some hundred priests, mostly Bretons, had made their home at Berwick, supported by monies paid out to them by Abbé Laennec, erstwhile Vicar General of Trequier, as agent of the Bishop of Saint-Pol-de-Léon. They played little rôle in Berwick society because of language difficulties and the suspicions of their neighbours. Some became French tutors and most frequented Catholic homes like Callaly Castle, Haggerston Castle and Berrington estate, and it was from Haggerston that in 1797 Fr. Michael Tidyman (1762-1832) called for 'procuring a chapel at Berwick'.

Little was to happen following Tidyman's call, but in 1816 the first permanent priest (probably Fr. William Pepper, OSB) arrived at Berwick, probably owing to the presence of the garrison during 1810-21 which helped increase the Catholic population. Rooms were used in a yard off Church Street for the saying of Mass. In 1829 Fr. William Birdsall (c.1785-1838) built the Roman Catholic Church used today, which is set behind 64 Ravensdowne and dedicated to Our Lady and St Cuthbert.

All the churches played their part in the education of the poor through their Sunday Schools, and a non-residential charity school was founded by Captain James Bolton in 1725 in the Back Way; here children were taught the Three Rs and church music. By 1886 the school was incorporated in the National system. A former sacking factory in Castlegate was reallocated in 1802 as a place where children were taught a trade, and this developed in conjunction with the Poor House. Associated with the Poor House was the town's Lunatic Asylum built in 1813.

Within the town the main property owners were the burgesses, the freemen and the tradesmen, while the properties within the boundaries to the north and west of the borough were owned by prominent families. These were the days when social welfare was very much a part of private philanthropy, and local landowners played a large part in charities associated with education, the church and the poor. By the late 1700s these families were the town's main benefactors, many of them taking up a long-established family responsibility: Mrs Bridge Watson Askew of Castlehills; Sir Francis Blake of Lethan; Walter Balderston of New Water Haugh; Robert Ogle of Gainslaw; Blake Stow Lundie of Bates Cross; Robert Romer of Cumberland Bower; George Hogarth of Halidon Hill and Marshall Meadows, and the ex-MP for Berwick, Wilmot Vaughan, the Earl of Lisburne who at this date owned Magdalene Fields. In his book on Berwick John Scott details charities started in Berwick for the benefit of the poor of which some of the most prominent were Valentine Mortoft's, Roger Tweedy's and Thomas Short's; Sir Robert Jackson, MP, had left money too for a House of Correction, 'for causing stubborn and idle people to be set on work'.

With the coming of the Napoleonic Wars (1798-1815) Berwick set up two companies of Volunteers who were joined by the privately-raised Loyal Masonic Volunteers, and Berwick was also an assembly point for the Sea Fencibles, the Hutton Trainbands and the Berwickshire Yeoman Cavalry. Although there were false alarms, the town had nothing to fear, but Goode's *Directory* shows military events reflected in the signs of Berwick public houses, from the Scotch Grey and the Volunteer to the Admiral St Vincent and the Gunner—in 1816 Berwick had sixty-four public houses for a population of 8600.

Feelings of gratitude and relief at the defeat of Napoleon led the better-off people in Berwick to found and open the Berwick Dispensary on 6 March 1814. It was designed to help the 'poor sick', but subscribers to the charity were allowed to nominate patients for treatment to the extent of their donations. Its first location was what is now 49 Church Street, and there it remained until 1826. Thereafter it moved to what is now the Custom House at 18 Quay Walls (see page 150). A public bath service was run at the Dispensary from 1820 to 1871. By the 1830s there was a growing public desire for an Infirmary, but this did not materialise until the present hospital was opened at Low Greens in 1874. Expansion took place in 1881, and in 1897 central heating was installed to celebrate Queen Victoria's Diamond Jubilee. The most celebrated Berwick medical practitioners were probably Dr George Johnston of 35 Woolmarket (The Anchorage), founder of the Berwickshire Naturalists' Club, and Dr Philip Whiteside Maclagen (d.1892). A memorial sculpture by D.W.Stevenson of Maclagen stood outside the newspaper offices in Marygate until it was sited in front of the Infirmary. A cholera hospital was set up in 1871 at Meadow Haven House, sponsored by the Berwick Shipping Co.

From the early 1800s Berwick depended far more on the rôle she was developing in providing food for the growing non-agricultural population than on her eighteenth-century base of small-scale industries. From the 1820s Berwick grew fast as a fishing port and as an exporter of agricultural produce from northern Northumberland and the Tweed Valley. Berwick Quay was extended and improved in the eighteenth and nineteenth centuries to cope with the output of the sawmills and the importing of iron and flax from Norway, and Baltic whale oil and tallow. There was a flourishing trade in salmon, eggs, pork, wool and grain too. The commonest vessels in the Tweed were the Berwick smacks of 120-150 tons, but there was much competition from French vessels plying the east coast, and the Leith merchantmen caused Berwick's fleet of smacks to dwindle by 1828. Some sailing vessels were built at Berwick and the shipyard established by Arthur Byram in 1751 was run by his family down to 1878. The yard closed in 1979 after a short-lived boost after World War II. The last of Berwick's clipper schooners, *The Thames*, was sold in 1869.

In 1802 a survey was made for a new pier at Berwick, and in 1808 an Act of Parliament was passed providing the wherewithal for its construction. This pier was to supersede its predecessors, the thirteenth-century Holdman Wall with its

A view of the Barracks and The Parade from the Cowport, the only surviving vaulted and portcullised gateway in the Elizabethan ramparts. Built 1595-96, the Cowport replaced the wooden Carey Port, and through this gateway the folk of Berwick led their cattle to the fields beyond in medieval times. The Parade was certainly in existence by 1610 and at the west end stood the Tudor King's Stables and the former Vicarage of *circa* 1749.

beacon of 1505, and the Queen Elizabeth Pier of 1577. The foundation stone was laid on 27 July 1810 and the pier was finished in 1821. On 17 February 1826 the foundation stone of the lighthouse was laid by Admiral Stow. Extra employment was offered to the town's labourers with the construction of the New Pier Road and the Riverside Walk.

By 1821 Berwick's new pattern for fairs and markets was established; markets were held every Wednesday and Saturday and three fairs were held, the first of the year being the second Wednesday in May for cattle and horses, and the others on the first Wednesday before 26 August and the first Wednesday in November. During mid-August 1822 George IV's royal yacht anchored in Berwick roads to refuel the steamer which was towing her, and the mayor and borough treasurer went out to the king's yacht on the coal tender to offer loyal greetings; they were not impressed by the cold buffet that the king offered for their sustenance and returned to the town disgruntled. This time the monarch was not saluted from the walls, as Berwick's cannon had been taken to Leith Fort in 1818.

In 1822 the borough was to be lit by gas lights using gas supplied by a company sited in Foul Ford; a rival gas company started at Spittal in 1844.

Change came with the passing of the Municipal Corporation Reform Act of 1835. The office of Sheriff, which had been entrusted to the mayor and bailiffs, now passed to an individual appointed by the council; the office of bailiff of the borough was also abolished. The power of 'life and death' was also stripped from the corporation by the Act of 1842 which now transferred capital offences to the Northumberland Assizes—the death sentence was last carried out at Berwick in 1823. Under William IV Berwick became 'a county in itself', and now on the king's death in 1837 it was about to enter a new era.

CHAPTER 10

Victorian and Edwardian Berwick

Berwick entered the Victorian Age at twelve minutes past two on the morning of 20 June 1837, the moment at which the last fitful spark of life was finally extinguished from the portly body of HRH Prince William Henry, the third son of George III and Queen Charlotte, who had ruled for seven years as King William IV. In Berwick a transformation was to be brought about with the coming of his niece as the new monarch, and this metamorphosis was to be felt in the town at all levels of society. Princess Georgina Charlotte Augusta Alexandrina Victoria, daughter of HRH Prince Edward, Duke of Kent, and HSH Mary Louisa Victoria of Saxe-Coburg-Saalfeld, was proclaimed Queen from an open window in St James's Palace on 21st June 1837, but it was to be thirteen years before her loyal subjects in Berwick took their first long look at their monarch, then aged thirty-one. This was to be the occasion of the opening of Berwick's largest and most important building project since the Elizabethan Walls had been commenced. The mighty Royal Border Bridge still takes the East Coast railway a bold 126 feet at its highest point across the River Tweed and the bridge, which looks so slender and fragile from a distance, is considered one of the great wonders of the railway world.

The Royal Border Bridge was formally opened on 29 August 1850 and Queen Victoria sealed the permanent railway link of the original East Coast route from London to Edinburgh. In 1844 a bill had been passed in Parliament for the making of a railway from Berwick to Edinburgh, and in 1846 this railway opened. In 1845 the new railway bridge was authorised and Robert Stephenson (1803-59), the English engineer and son of the celebrated George Stephenson, designed the bridge for the Newcastle and Berwick Railway—this company amalgamated in 1847 with its southern neighbour, the York and Newcastle Railway, as the York, Newcastle and Berwick Railway. On 2

September 1848 a temporary wooden structure, which had been started in February, was completed and thus the terminus of the North British Railway was linked across the Tweed with the YN&BR, using 90,000 ft of timber and at a cost of £2900. The stone bridge was built alongside this structure.

The vital statistics of the masonry and stone bridge are that it runs to 28 semi-circular arches, each of 61ft.6in span, and a length of 2160 ft. Its greatest height from the bed of the river to the parapets is 126ft.6in, and its width between the parapets is 24ft. Some 1,437,000 cubic feet of masonry and 1,750,000 bricks were used, and the stone came from Northumbrian quarries. During the construction some 2738 men and 180 horses were engaged on the work which included piling-up 700,000 cubic yards of soil to make the great sweeping embankment at the Tweedmouth approach. Messrs Mackay & Blackstock of Cumberland secured the contract for the bridge which, with its approaches, was to cost £263,000.

The foundations of the bridge piers, kept dry in coffer dams pumped out by 50hp steam engines and driven into the sand and gravel of the river bed by two of Nasmyth's steam piling hammers, took two years to construct. The first stone of the foundations of the bridge was laid on 15 May 1847 by Mrs G.B.Bruce, the wife of the resident bridge engineer. The Newcastle to Tweedmouth railway was completed on 1 July 1847 and Tweedmouth was linked with the North British Railway station at Berwick in the interim by an omnibus service over the Old Bridge.

The 1200ft long temporary wooden bridge was brought into use on 10 October 1848 and Queen Victoria crossed this structure during September 1849 on her way to London from Balmoral. The last arch of the stone bridge was keyed on 26 March 1850 and a single track was used for goods trains from 20 July, and the first passenger service began on 1 August 1850. The *Berwick Advertiser* detailed the opening ceremony. The 31 August 1850 issue noted that between 10,000 and 12,000 people packed the town on the day of opening and the pilot engine running ahead of the royal train arrived shortly after 3

The Royal Border Bridge was formally opened on 29 August 1850 and Queen Victoria sealed the permanent railway link of the original East Coast route from London to Edinburgh. The bridge has 28 semi-circular spans, each of 61ft 6in, and runs to a length of 2160ft. Messrs Mackay and Blackstock of Cumberland secured the contract for the bridge which, with its approaches, was to cost £263,000 (*Neil Potts*).

pm. to pass over the bridge around 3.05 pm. On the platform of Berwick station to meet the Queen, Prince Albert and four of the royal children were Earl Grey, Sir George Grey and the chief officers of the railway. The party were seated in a specially prepared pavilion, and there the Royal Family received formal addresses from the mayor and sheriff. The Queen spoke of the admiration she had for the bridge and requested that it be called the Royal Border Bridge although it did not unite the two countries of England and Scotland. The royal party departed around 3.15 pm to continue their journey north, while the town celebrated until the early hours of the next day. Since then the bridge has never undergone any major structural alteration and there is no weight restriction on current traffic; the fabric is examined regularly and binoculars are used to study the more inaccessible parts of the spans and piers.

A two-carriage local train crosses the Royal Border Bridge to Berwick
station, *circa* 1910. Salmon fishing boats line the north shore of the
Tweed and the New Road, constructed some time after the
Napoleonic Wars, bisects the Water Tower. The White Wall climbs
left to the station level; the wall incidentally escaped demolition in
1720 when stone was required to build the Barracks (*Henry Kerr*).

Berwick's railway station is still a focal point of the northern
approach to the town. The North British Railway purchased the
ruined site of Berwick Castle for their railway in 1843, and by
the Act of 1844 the company was 'incorporated for the
construction of a railway from Edinburgh to Berwick with a
branch to Haddington, in all 62 miles, and on 22 June 1846,

The original mock-gothic facade of Berwick station *circa* 1900. The station was first built on the site of Berwick Castle by the North British Railway Co, 1844-46, as the terminus of the Berwick-Edinburgh line; the station was rebuilt 1924-27 and has since been renovated. Today the coal yard on the right is a car park (*The Estate of M.I. Johnston*).

when the line was opened for traffic, Berwick station came into being', wrote Frederick Stoton for *Railway Magazine*.

Before its reconstruction Berwick station was bisected by the road bridge into two large complexes; looking north, the passenger station, goods yard (largely dismantled) and grain store (demolished) were on the site of the castle, whereas the engine shed, the horse and cattle loading bay and the marshalling sidings were on the site of the Tapee loch. The old station buildings were in the Scottish baronial style, and the siting was a piece of Victorian audacity in its destruction of the medieval castle, although the latter was badly ruined. Some station reconstruction was carried out during 1916-21, and the station works were not restarted until 1924-27 because of World War I. The work included completely new passenger services, signalling equipment and luggage hoists. Today's station facade is largely that of 1924-27, but the original Railway

Street goods yard and goods shed have been converted into a
car park.

The new Victorian architects quickly established their mark
in Berwick. Neo-classical houses and neo-Gothic churches
began to jostle with medieval and Hanoverian relics. Sound,
functional, yet opulent Victorian dwellings were erected which
still stand as a memorial to the go-getting commercial
prosperity of the age.

One of the major building projects of the era, after the Royal
Border Bridge was built, was the erection of St Mary's Anglican
church at the top of Castlegate. Designed to serve the fishing
community of the Greenses, its foundation stone was laid on 20
October 1857 by Charles Thomas Longley, Bishop of Durham,
who consecrated the church on 23 November 1858. It was to be
the northernmost church in England and cost £2500, the main
donor being Capt. Charles W. Gordon. The Victorian Gothic
church contains the 'Fishermen's Transept'. The church
school to serve the Greenses was opened in 1866 and closed in
1972 when a new school was opened at the north end of
Berwick. Outside the church is Berwick war memorial designed
by Alexander Carrick. There are a few houses off Castlegate
which were embellished with nineteenth-century stone carved
figures, the work of William Wilson of Tweedmouth, at 11
Railway Street and 48 Tweed Street (formerly Windmillhole).
The British Infants' School (which possibly gave its name to
College Street) on the Walls dates from 1840 and the early
Victorian architectural drive in Berwick.

The average Victorian middle-class Berwicker's character
was one of sober morality founded on the gospel of self-help. By
the time Edward came to the throne in 1901 they had become
immensely conscious of social divisions and they found great
satisfaction in their corporate identity. By and large the middle-
class Berwick burgess was a Gladstonian Liberal, and family life
in Victorian and Edwardian Berwick centred on the church.
Sunday was a sterile day of well-worn ritual: family and servants
(the latter when duties permitted) repaired to church or kirk,
and all were dressed in decorous greys and blacks.

The vegetable and fruit market, Marygate, *circa* 1876. Berwick's weekly markets have a long history and the annual May Fair was first mentioned in a royal charter of 1302. The town houses of the eighteenth and nineteenth centuries are clearly seen in a thoroughfare uncluttered by traffic. Street trading remained an important source of domestic goods until at least the end of the First World War (*W.A. Montgomery*).

Berwick was a noisy scene in Victorian and Edwardian days, with the wheels of carriages and the horses in drays being the noisiest as they clattered over the cobbles. People went about their business from the early hours. Busy indeed, but the wages were low: at Hide Hill and Sandgate on the 'Hiring Days' in, say, 1902, the farm labourer was negotiating a weekly wage of 19/- (95p) a week.

For entertainment there was the pub, the church soirée, a concert at the Corn Exchange or the laughter brought by a visiting troupe. That curious little man, Charles Stratton (1838-83), the US midget billed as 'General Tom Thumb', was a favourite with the crowds when he came to Berwick in 1867 and 1871. And then there was the famous Mr Charles Dickens who gave readings in 1858 and 1861 and is commemorated by a plaque outside the King's Arms Hotel.

Eating out was not as common as it is today, but by the 1800s Berwick's ladies of 'good reputation' could dine at last in public and the tea shop was all the rage, Berwick being well served by such as J.J.Simmen of 31 Bridge Street with his 'French and English Confectionery' which opened for business in 1884. It was an age of mobility. The reorganisation of industry brought an influx of strangers into the town and general trade flourished in Victorian and Edwardian Berwick. Several of Berwick's businesses of the 1980s had their foundations in Victorian Berwick and earlier. For instance Messrs Paxton & Purves, now in the High Street, were established in Western Lane in 1802 by John Paxton, and by 1888 they had expanded into old Scotsgate House with a fine emporium as drapers and silk mercers. At 64-66 Bridge Street are Messrs Wm.Cowe & Sons, who had a grocery shop in Marygate in 1801; they bought Weatherheads in Bridge Street in 1886, and won fame for their 'Original Berwick Cockles'; their wholesale department at Victorian Buildings is on the site of John Wilson & Son, the prominent Victorian Border ironmongers. Further along the street are the fishmongers Ralph Holmes & Sons, established in 1760, and the name of H.G.McCreath has been associated with the Border grain business since the 1880s.

Freemasonry began in Berwick in the eighteenth century and played an important rôle in the life of the town. Before 1828 the history of masonic lodges in Berwick is confused, but it seems that from 1773 there was a permanent presence in the town. Lodges came and went, but the records of the movement give the local historian some good clues as to the social scene in eighteenth and nineteenth-century Berwick. For instance the masons met in various Berwick hostelries, many of which have now vanished—some met at the White Bear, Kid's Hill in 1774, and others at the Angel, High Street. St David's Lodge met at the Gibraltar Tavern in 1794 and at the Red Lion in 1802, but by 1828, when a new warrant was subscribed for their lodge, they met at the Berwick Arms. Clearly the masons did not have a permanent home until their hall was built in the Parade; constructed as a masonic lodge, it was dedicated on 30 January

1874 and cost £3000.

St David's Lodge has an interesting collection of ephemera which reflect Berwick's history. The collection includes the *Vexillum Belli* and the *Beauceant* (War Cry of the Knights of the Temple), two banners said to have been sent from Wark to Berwick for safe keeping, during the unsettled times which culminated in the Battle of Flodden. Like the many Scottish Standards and English Banners carried that day in August 1513, they may have been held aloft at the charge by masons within the opposing armies. There is also a marble tablet found at the north-east corner of Tweedmouth Church with the inscription: 'This church foundation was laid Dec 27, 1782, by the Rt Worshipful Master Salby Morton of the Lodge of St Cuthberts 133'. St Cuthbert's was a lodge of Freemasons in Tweedmouth. Within St David's too is a chair of 1733 from earlier lodges and a chair dated 1641 set with masonic symbols. Masons were present at the laying of the foundation stone of Berwick Pier, and an apron worn by James Good on that day, 27 July 1810, is on display, as is the apron worn by the surveyor of Berwick Pier, Brother John Fox. The collection includes several fine snuffboxes of wood and silver and the snuffbox reputed to have been made of wood from Berwick's medieval bridge. Among the banners at the lodge is that of the 8th and King's Regiment presented to St Cuthbert's Lodge, 1806; it is known that the masons had their own corps of volunteers during the Napoleonic Wars, who acted as a defence force to the town. Here too is a picture of the mouth of the Tweed showing the location of the fleet when George IV visited Scotland.

The mayor and bailiffs of Berwick were responsible for law and order in the town from 1603 to the Municipal Corporation Reform Act of 1835; before 1603 the duties of keeping the peace were largely the responsibility of the governor, although the mayor and bailiffs co-operated out of self-interest. The history of the police in Berwick developed from Sir Robert Peel's reorganisation of the Metropolitan Police Force in 1829. During 1833 parishes were empowered to elect inspectors and appoint watchmen, and the Municipal Corporation Reform Act of 1835 required every borough to appoint a watch committee with a duty of instituting a police force; the local force was amalgamated with that of the County of Northumberland in 1920. There was a House of Correction in Berwick during the seventeenth-century on the site of the Tudor Stables facing the Parade (later the site for the Girls' and Infants' National School of 1856 and the present public library). A jail (now the Borough Council Offices) had been built during 1848-49 at Wallace Green at a cost of £8500 to replace the lock-up at the Town Hall, and a police and magistrates' court was erected in 1899-1901; the police station in Church Street was built in 1900. Summary justice, of course, had been handed out at Gallows Knowe (at the foot of today's Castle Terrace), and the last person to be hanged there was Janet Griffin in the early nineteenth century.

During 1867 Berwick received a threat from the Fenians (a secret society of Irishmen whose aims were to bring about the separation of Ireland from England and the establishment of an Irish Republic), and a detachment of the 72nd Highlanders was sent to Berwick to protect the barracks on which an attack was expected. No attack occurred. But the regiment that is most closely associated with the town is the King's Own Scottish Borderers. In 1881 the KOSBs moved to Berwick and the depot was closed in 1963 when the regiment moved to Glencorse Barracks, Edinburgh, but the regimental headquarters remained in the town, and this, with the museum of the KOSBs, which has a very fine collection of military regalia, is situated in 'O' Block, the original officers' quarters, and in 'A' Block (see page 203).

Berwick celebrated Queen Victoria's two great jubilees of 1887 and 1897, and the borough's streets were hung with bunting and the public buildings decorated. Private houses, too, were decorated to show the loyalty of the residents. There were processions from the Town Hall to the parish church on both occasions, and the Berwick school children, who were given a holiday, had their processions too. There were various projects in the town to celebrate the great events (see page 130).

The Edwardian Age began at six-thirty in the evening of 23

Seamen chat at Berwick quay, *circa* 1900. The town's quay was first limited to the area immediately below the Old Bridge, although a medieval quay area probably stretched as far as the boathouse. Berwick's quay was extended and updated in the late eighteenth and early nineteenth centuries. Downstream was Arthur Byram's shipyard, famous for the construction of the Berwick smacks which carried passengers and goods between Leith, Berwick and London (*The Estate of M.I. Johnston*).

January 1901, when Queen Victoria died at Osborne House, Isle of Wight. The reign of the portly and fun-loving Edward VII was to inherit the sombre colours of his mother's reign, quite out of keeping with his own character. By the time Edward himself died on 6 May 1910 at a quarter to midnight at Buckingham Palace, Berwick had seen a great deal of change. The Berwicker born in 1837 and dying in 1910 would have seen the spread of popular education, an increase in mobility through the new transport systems, and the development of trade unionism, especially amongst the unskilled, which was to make lasting changes in society. Berwick's Edwardian middle class entrenched themselves in new houses in Northumberland Avenue and the Castlegate, and for many there was peace and plenty, but all this was to be shattered by the guns of Mons, and prosperity was drowned in the mud of Flanders.

CHAPTER 11

Modern Berwick

By far the most ambitious project in Berwick between the wars was the construction of the Royal Tweed Bridge, known colloquially as the New Bridge, which was opened by HRH Prince Edward, Prince of Wales, in 1928. Designed by Mouchel & Partners and built by Holloway Bros., the £180,000 bridge carried the Great North Road over the Tweed and into the heart of Berwick. Four spans of reinforced concrete vault the Tweed and cross the public path on the Berwick side called the New Road, from which perhaps the best views of Berwick's three bridges can be had. A feat of engineering maybe, but the Royal Tweed Bridge was a disaster: it increased the weight of traffic trundling through Berwick to an intolerable degree; it destroyed Golden Square and, while relieving traffic over the Old Bridge, as modern traffic levels increased it helped clog Marygate, particularly during the summer, and threatened the Scotsgate with demolition every time an extra large lorry passed through it. Berwick had to wait fifty-five years for a bypass.

From the 1930s to the 1960s Berwick endured a kind of slow decay. The modern heart of Berwick was and is predominantly eighteenth century and conforms still to the medieval street plan. Yet in the eighteenth century all traces of medieval town building were removed, and development began to the north and west (the suburbs of Castlegate and the Greenses). The Victorian and Edwardian eras saw expansion into Castle Terrace and North Road, which had developed by the 1930s and 1940s into a mixture of private and municipal housing schemes.

A significant spur to Berwick's modern development happened in 1926, the year in which the Berwick-upon-Tweed Corporation (Freemen) Act was passed. The powers and privileges of the old Guild members (or freemen) had been taken away by the Municipal Corporation Reform Act of 1835,

The Royal Tweed Bridge, known colloquially as the New Bridge, was designed by L.G. Mouchel and Partners 1925-28. Some 1410ft long, the £180,000 bridge carried the A1(Great North Road) on a new route into the heart of Berwick. Four spans of reinforced concrete vault the Tweed; one of the spans is 361ft. The bridge was opened in 1928 by the then Prince of Wales (*Neil Potts*).

but with the passing of the 1926 Act the Guild was revived with its own committee and trustees, and a new set of privileges and rules was established. By the nineteenth century the property held by the mayor, bailliffs and burgesses of Berwick—as defined by the 1604 charter—was defined in the four categories mentioned within *Notes for the guidance and information of The Freemen of the Borough of Berwick-Upon-Tweed* (1968): 'The first of these was made up of 333 unequal parcels of land termed "meadows" held for their own benefit on a basis of seniority by 333 resident freemen or freemen's widows. The second consisted of land leased out, the rent of which was split up in shares of "Stints in Lieu of Meadows" for 163 freemen or widows for whom there were no meadows available. The third consisted of more land leased out, the rent of which was first subject to a local rate for Borough purposes, and then split up in shares or "stints" for all 496 freemen who participated in the

On 16 May 1928, HRH Edward, Prince of Wales, visited Berwick for the opening of the new four-span reinforced concrete Royal Tweed Bridge. The picture shows the Prince's entry into Berwick over the Old Bridge and into the then cobbled Bridge Street, the congestion of which the new bridge was designed to alleviate (*The Estate of M.I. Johnston*).

first and second parts. The fourth comprised a number of "Treasurer's Farms", whose rent provided the money for the salaries of some town officials, and other expenses including a number of ancient charities, among them the maintenance of the Corporation Academy'.

　　In 1835 all of these properties were handed over to the newly elected Town Council, which maintained the rights of the freemen, and in fact the freemen continued to occupy their meadows and receive their 'stints'. By 1918 the terms of the Freeman Act of 1843 endorsing the previous rights were proving a serious drawback to the development of the borough, and the new Act of 1926 invested the existing properties in two bodies, the Corporation (Freemen) Trustees and a Freeman's Committee. These bodies still exist and the Freemen Trustees still hold extensive properties (or monies from the sale of

The Lions House is an early nineteenth-century dwelling which occupies a prominent site by the Elizabethan Walls. By 1971 it was in this dilapidated state and would have been demolished if it had not been presented to the Town Preservation Trust, itself formed in 1971. The Trust later transferred the house to three local businessmen who restored it.

properties for instance in locations like Castle Terrace) within the borough. The monies are divided between the Freemen and the modern Council. At the moment a resolution has been passed by the Council to promote a Private Act of Parliament to alter the Constitution of the Freeman Estates to win a larger slice of the profits from the estates.

The Lions on the gateway of the early nineteenth-century Lions House are a distinctive feature of Berwick's architectural curiosities. Originally the lions were painted red, white and bronze. The banner of the Lion of Scotland, incidentally, last flew over Berwick marking Scottish ownership in 1482 when the town was taken for the English by Richard, Duke of Gloucester, who was soon to rule as Richard III (*Neil Potts*).

Berwick-upon-Tweed Preservation Trust was formed in 1971 and from its beginnings set about the task of restoring six properties which had been listed as of historic or architectural importance. These were:

12 Quay Walls, rebuilt.

13 Quay Walls, rebuilt and outside ironwork replaced during European Architectural Heritage Year (1975).

5 Quay Walls (now Collingwood House) of *circa* 1790, rebuilt 1975-76.

The Lions House, Windmill Hill, an early nineteenth-century dwelling, was restored by local businessmen: the lion sculptures which give the house its name were formerly painted in red, white and bronze.

A panoramic view of Berwick showing the Victorian and Edwardian development of Castle Terrace rising on the north bank of the Tweed. In the left foreground Berwick's swans rest and feed in their favourite haunt by the bridges. The town's mute swans — so called because they make little noise compared with the Whooper and Bewick swans — are the only ones to nest in Britain (*Neil Potts*).

20 Quay Walls, renovated 1975; the basement revealed openings into the Elizabethan defences against which the house sits.

The Granary, purchased by the Anchor Housing Trust who demolished it in 1978-79 and erected flats for the aged to blend with the environs.

The initial work of the Trust was to make sure that these six properties were restored in such a way as to fit the modern environment and be brought back into habitable use. An underlying idea too was, through such work, to encourage others to renovate derelict properties.

The Trust now turned to:

30 Ravensdowne— 'ice-house' cottages of *circa* 1790— restored into a single house 1978-79.

21 Quay Walls, a fine mid-eighteenth century house, with two Venetian windows on each of its upper floors and a

Part of the Quay Walls showing the restored facade of the Custom House with its flagpole. This eighteenth-century building was restored by the Property Services Agency for its owners, the Department of the Environment. The Custom House was formerly a private house, used from 1826 to 1872 as the town Dispensary (a forerunner of the Infirmary) (*Neil Potts*).

splendid doorway, which was the home of the Berwick artist Thomas Sword Good.

The Custom House, Quay Walls, which was restored by the Property Services Agency; from 1826-72 it was the old Dispensary of the town, the precursor of Berwick Infirmary.

Sailors' Barracks, Palace Green, demolished and new houses built.

A myriad of houses in Church Street, West End, Tweedmouth, Wallace Green, Ravensdowne, West Street and so on have been renovated and recent projects have included the seventeenth-century property at 12 Palace Green; numbers 25-27 Palace Green were the home of Arthur Byram, shipowner, and the property was renovated in 1982.

The Preservation Trust entered another phase in 1986 with the launch of a new appeal, and further projects were

L.S. Lowry's (1887-1976) 'Berwick-on-Tweed' of 1938, showing Bridgend leading to the foot of West Street at its junction with Love Lane and Bridge Street. Lowry was a frequent visitor to Berwick and also painted 'Old Berwick' (*circa* 1956) showing the Town Hall, and 'At Berwick' (1961) depicting the steps at Sally Port (*Ronald Lyon*).

undertaken. One such was the renovation and conversion into residential and office accommodation of 3 Quay Walls. Much has been done too in the town by private individuals buying old properties and 'doing them up' for their own use, and companies too have helped to reshape old Berwick. The Boots building in Marygate, for example, was built in the 1970s on the site of the Waterloo Hotel and Taylor's the butchers.

Swans, sweets and a ship have long been associated with Berwick and are a part of today's image of the town. The swan has a special place among Berwick's fauna, for the bridges at Berwick are the favourite haunt of the town's mute swans. The mute swans—so called because they make little noise compared with Whooper or Bewick swans—are the only ones to nest in Britain (the others being winter visitors). Incidentally

Marygate on market day; Berwick still holds markets on Wednesdays and Saturdays. Subject to much redevelopment, this part of Berwick exhibits the tradenames of major high street traders as well as long-established Berwick businesses (*Neil Potts*)

Northumberland County Council National Parks and Countryside Department have prepared a two-mile nature trail in Berwick which starts at Castlegate car park, where a free leaflet about the trail can be obtained at the town's information centre.

Berwick's name is still retained in the boiled sweet, 'Berwick Cockles'. It originated as a home-made sweet but became so popular that it was produced commercially. The rights to produce the true Berwick Cockle are still held by Messrs. Wm. Cowe of 64-66 Bridge Street, who have made the sweet on the premises since 1801. The name is derived from the sweet's cockle shape.

From time to time HMS *Berwick* anchored off Berwick-upon-Tweed and there were friendly get-togethers between townsfolk and crew. HMS *Berwick* (F115) was a 2380-ton vessel of the 6th Frigate Squadron and was of the 'Rothesay' Class and was built by Harland & Wolff in 1958. HMS *Berwick* was the tenth ship to bear the name, the first being a 1089-ton 70-gunner of 1679. HMS *Berwick* (F115) was paid off in 1985, and sunk as a target in the North Atlantic in August 1986.

Berwick has always been proud of its international associations. Historians talk, for instance, of how the craftsman Caleb Buglass (1738-97) of Woolmarket became a skilled bookbinder, and some of his work entered George Washington's library. And on 15 June 1982 the Borough of Berwick-upon-Tweed became a 'sister city' of the City of Berwick, Australia. So Berwick has come a long way from being medieval Scotland's most prominent burgh to a 'sister' of a Commonwealth town less than a hundred years old.

Still today the folk of Berwick are themselves as *apart* from both Scotland and England as they ever were; they are geographically and administratively *a part* of England but do not belong in spirit or inclination to either a Celtic or an Anglo-Saxon culture: they are almost a 'nationality' in themselves— they are Berwick folk first and Britons second.

CHAPTER 12

The Manor of Tweedmouth

W.Armstrong's map of 1769 shows clearly how Tweedmouth had developed by the eighteenth-century. There was one long, irregular street of houses joined to Berwick by the seventeenth-century bridge, and corresponding to modern West End and Main Street. West End was linked via the site of the development of modern West End Road to Ord Road (the A698) and the village of East Ord. Main Street led into High Gate and Belford Road and forked, as it still does, into a road to Ord Moor (via the line of modern Shielfield Terrace). Two toll houses controlled the road south, High Gate and Low Gate; one of Tweedmouth's old toll houses can be seen at 27 Main Street. Kiln Hill led up to dwellings that were to be divided by the modern A1. To the south of Tweedmouth was Spittal (Spittle in the eighteenth century) Common and all around was a desolate moorland which had been the haunt of lawless gypsies in medieval times, but by the eighteenth century there was some farming. 'Travelling folk' still have a link with Tweedmouth with their caravan park at Main Street. Armstrong's map shows a windmill on the site of modern Mill Farm, and in this area brown earthenware pots and bricks were manufactured. By this time, too, Sunnyside was a military training area.

It is certain that two areas of Tweedmouth were developed first: the environs of the parish church and the south end of the bridge. Records show that Tweedmouth parish church was probably founded during the pontificate of the Blessed Eugene III (1145-53), who was well known in England for his support of Archbishop Theobald of Canterbury against King Stephen, and his ejection of (St) William Fitzherbert from the see of York. In these days Tweedmouth church was a chapel within the parish of Holy Island, dedicated to St Boisil (St Boswell). Boisil had trained for the priesthood under St Aidan and was a monk of Mailros (Melrose). A biblical scholar and preacher of note, Boisil succeeded St Eata as Abbot of Mailros; as Prior of Melrose he had received St Cuthbert into holy orders. Boisil died of plague in 664 and his feast day was celebrated at Tweedmouth on 23 February. The parish church was rebuilt in 1783, and some time before 1793 the dedication was changed to St Bartholomew, whose name had been associated with the leper hospital at Spittal (see page 166). During the rebuilding of the church the floor level was raised and a nave with west gallery, a tower and a north transept were constructed. Additions were carried out in 1841 and in 1866 a gothicisation took place when the chancel was enlarged and a vestry added (the vestry was removed in 1878). The living of Tweedmouth was in the gift of the Dean and Chapter of Durham and was given to a perpetual curate (a living which had no endowment of tithes). In 1868 the post was changed to that of vicar.

The cemetery around St Bartholomew's parish church is crammed with intriguing tabletombs and monuments in memory of Tweedmouth and Spittal fisher families. One tombstone (now vanished) was long pointed out as commemorating James Stuart, nicknamed 'Jimmy Strength'. A contemporary description of this eccentric ran thus: 'This extraordinary character . . . completed his One Hundred and Fourteenth year on Christmas 1842. He is a son of General John Stuart and grandson of the Lady Airlie in Scottish song, who was taken out of her own house at Airlie by a party of the clan Campbell, and killed. He was a witness of the Battle of Culloden, and indeed claims kindred with the Pretender himself, whose name he bears. He was at the battle of Bunkers Hill, and held an ensigncy in General Wolfe's army and was present at Quebec when that distinguished officer was killed. He has been five times married, and is the father of no less than 27 children, 10 of whom have been killed fighting the battles of their country in different parts of the world. Before declining age overtook him he was a phenomenon of personal strength, so much so as to entitle him to the name of "Jamie Strength" by which he is generally known in the neighbourhood of Berwick.

He still retains his memory unimpaired, and is an object of great interest'. All of these titbits entered Berwick folklore but they are based on fancy rather than reality, even though they were given some public credence by William Howitt (1792-1879), the celebrated 'miscellaneous writer', in his *Visit to Remarkable Places* (1855). In truth Stuart probably suffered from scoliosis and dwarfism and was one of the many characterful itinerants who haunted the Borders up to the present time. He was certainly not 'grandson of the Lady Airlie in Scottish song'—she was Lady Helen Ogilvy (d.1664), daughter of James Ogilvy, Earl of Airlie (1586-1664), and was wife of Sir John Carnegy of Balnamoon. They had one son and no grandchildren called John Stuart. The song referred to is 'The Bonny House of Airlie' which tells of the attack on Airlie Castle by the Covenanting Archibald Campbell, Earl of Argyll, in July 1640. It is possible that James Stuart was a witness of Culloden in 1746, but his stature is unlikely to have offered him an ensigncy (until 1871 the lowest officer rank) at the Battle of Bunker Hill in 1775 during the American Revolution; General James Wolfe was killed in 1759 during the siege of Quebec. James Stuart died on 11 April 1844 and a statue of him by the Tweedmouth sculptor John Wilson (once to be found at Bayview House and moved in 1978) used to stand in Palace Green, Berwick.

In Tweedmouth parish church graveyard too is buried John Mackay Wilson (1804-35), another Tweedmouth character worthy of note. The son of a Tweedmouth millwright, Wilson was educated at the Presbyterian school in the village and after spending a short time as an assistant at a Berwick school became an apprentice compositor with the printer William Lochhead. Wilson published several poems in the *Tyne Mercury* during 1823-24 and in 1824 published his first book, *A Glance at Hinduism*. On moving to London after his apprenticeship at Berwick had come to an end, Wilson experienced great hardship and returned to Berwick. By 1829 he was working for the Edinburgh *Literary Journal* and tried his hand at writing stage plays. In March 1832 he was appointed editor of the *Berwick*

W. Finden's steel engraving, 'Berwick-on-Tweed from the South East', was used as an illustration for Dr James Taylor's *The Pictorial History of Scotland* (1859). It also shows Tweedmouth foreshore and the stations of the salmon fishers. Recently salmon net fishing on the Tweed has been cut under a conservation scheme arranged by the Atlantic Salmon Conservation Trust.

Advertiser. By far his most important and best-known work is his *Tales of the Borders* which appeared for the first time in their threehalfpenny numbers on 8 November 1834. They were the local 'bestsellers' of the day and Wilson published forty-eight numbers in all comprising seventy-three tales. His story 'The Poor Scholar' had autobiographical overtones. It is thought that the strain of editing a weekly newspaper and producing a weekly journal of stories caused his death on 2 October 1835. Wilson's *Tales* continued to be reprinted throughout the nineteenth century.

The development of the area around the modern bridge end of Tweedmouth and Union Brae predated the parish church. From early times it was a resting place for travellers and those who had to stay the night when the bridge gate was closed after curfew. The town gates were closed at 8.00 pm every day and opened again at 5.00 am; both activities were signalled by the tolling of bells. Down the centuries there have been several taverns at the bridge end. The white-fronted house (opposite the war memorial and now an old people's home) is prominent today as 4 Main Street and was once the Virgin Inn, run by Hannah Humphreys and her sisters. In this eighteenth-century house stayed the novelist and erstwhile surgeon, Tobias

Smollett (1721-71), when travelling with his wife and Miss Anne
Curry in the Spring of 1766 on the journey which produced
material for his *Expedition of Humphry Clinker* (1771), in which,
within 'Matt Bramble's letter of 15 July to Dr Lewis', Smollett
left this impression of Northumberland:

> Northumberland is a fine county, extending to the Tweed, which is a
> pleasant pastoral stream; but you will be surprised when I tell you that the
> English side of that river is neither so well cultivated nor so populous as the
> other. The farms are thinly scattered, the lands unenclosed, and scarce a
> gentleman's seat is to be seen in some miles from the Tweed; whereas the
> Scots are advanced in crowds to the very brink of the river; so that you may
> reckon above thirty good houses, in the compass of a few miles, belonging
> to proprietors whose ancestors had fortified castles in the same situations;
> a circumstance that shows what dangerous neighbours the Scots must
> have formerly been to the northern counties of England.

Smollett went on to describe Berwick as having 'a tolerable
market'; he talks of 'a frightful moor' between Berwick and
Dunbar, and in Berwick he observed that Northumbrians were
'boors' and the Scots 'lusty fellows' and 'generally lank, lean,
hard-featured, sallow, solid and shabby'. In the section 'To Sir
Watkin Phillips, Bart . . . To Melford, 18 July', Smollett
describes his Tweedmouth hostess Mrs Humphreys as 'a very
good sort of a woman'. Today the house where he stayed retains
its supposed priest hole.

Next to the house where Smollett stayed was the former
Rising Sun public house at 1 West End, and nearby under the
Royal Tweed Bridge is Pudding Lane which led in Smollett's
day to the Fields of Tweedmouth. The buildings in West End
were renewed by the Borough Council in the mid-1970s, but
the old Thatch Inn recalls the earlier hostelry age; the mounting
block ('louping stane' in local parlance) outside the present pub
is all that remains of the tavern of 1535. The original tavern was
burned down in 1886 and in this former building were paid the
merchants who had brought materials for the seventeenth-century bridge's construction. Parliament Close across the way
recalls a Parliament of Edward I said to have been held hereabouts in 1279; in reality it was a meeting (site now forgotten)
between Scottish and English commissioners met to reconcile

Border disputes. Just by the Victorian railway bridge is the knoll called Hang-a-Dyke-Neuk (see page 60). The older buildings at 20-32 West End were built by Mackay and Blackstock, who constructed the Royal Border Bridge, and were used as stables, stores and offices; in the 1850s they were converted into dwellings and earned the name 'Tommy' (tally) shops where goods were exchanged for credit tickets for sums to be deducted from the wages (with interest) of the railway navvies.

King John—as part of his assault on Berwick—fortified a castle at Tweedmouth in 1204 and entrusted the work to Philip, Bishop of Durham. William I of Scotland, however, caused the half-built castle to be demolished as it was a threat to his fortress at Berwick. It is thought that the castle was in the area of modern Mount Road. Nearby, in today's Tower Road, stood Tweedmouth Tower, mentioned as being 'in reasonable good reparocions' in the early sixteenth century, but by 1560 it had vanished. It is said that the original tower was within the policies of the leper hospital at Spittal, and in the thirteenth century the hospital administrator, called Bather, may have built it—what remained of the tower was still called after him in the seventeenth century.

In the eighteenth and nineteenth centuries Tweedmouth developed as a place of coal pits (Tweedmouth Moor), stone quarries, brick fields, pantileries and earthenware vessel manufactories. William Walker & Co. established a tannery at Tweedmouth in 1787 carrying on an already established business, and in 1795 a tannery to turn sheepskin into leather had been established in Tweedmouth by Mark Young who also processed wool to be taken by cart from Tweedmouth to the looms at Wooler, Kelso, Jedburgh, Selkirk, Galashiels and Dalkeith. Tweedmouth was also known for its horn spoons (James Tait's workshops, *circa* 1785), starch making (Selby Morton, *circa* 1798) and the manufacture of red herrings (1797), that cured and dried fish which entered the language as a euphemism for a diversionary tactic.

With the building of the railway, industry developed further and Tweedmouth's major employers included the Border

Brewery Co., Black's Boiler Works, Wilson's the Masons, and Short's Grain Mill erected in 1877 on the site of an oil seed crushing mill and a *papier-mâché* mill. Founded in the eighteenth century, the Border Brewery drew on Tweedmouth's mineral springs which had been celebrated since medieval times. Ladywell Road in Tweedmouth still recalls the Holy Well of the Blessed Virgin situated nearby. Probably the oldest boiler works in the North of England, Black's were founded in 1790 in Main Street (close to the railway embankment by the bridge) and the firm were celebrated for their 'Lancashire, Cornish, multitubular, vertical and loco-type steel boilers' exported as far away as China. John Wilson's monumental works were situated at Bridge End and their work is to be seen in local graveyards and gardens; they made the Caen stone altar for Berwick's Roman Catholic church. Wilson's was on the site of a shipyard run by Joseph Todd, *circa* 1799-1810; two small warships, HMS *Forward* and HMS *Rover*, were built here and saw service in the Napoleonic Wars. Today the work is kept on by A. & J. Robertson (Granite) Ltd. Tweedmouth was also a north-eastern centre for the manufacture of clay pipes and 80-84 Main Street was the site of Tennant's Clay Pipe Factory.

The development of the railway at Tweedmouth should not be underestimated. Tweedmouth was linked into a railway system that stretched across a large part of southern Scotland, and was an important junction on the East Coast route. It was an important locomotive depot with a marshalling yard, a ramp for the coaling waggons and a brakedown crane. At one time Tweedmouth station housed a large variety of engines and was the base for a 'standing pilot', an engine used to help failed locomotives return to depot. By 1923 there were forty-four ex-North Eastern Railway locomotives at Tweedmouth, and in 1924 the North Eastern Railway amalgamated with the North British Railway. A station had been built in 1847, a motive power depot was developed from the same year, and the Berwick and Kelso Railway was developed via Tweedmouth when the Royal Border Bridge was opened (see page 33). The passenger service from Berwick/Tweedmouth to Kelso ceased in June 1964; the line was closed in its entirety on 29 March 1965 and thereafter Tweedmouth station was dismantled. Incidentally a railway had led to Tweedmouth much earlier, as a waggonway from the mines at Unthank was operational by 1764.

Besides its parish church, Tweedmouth catered for other religious denominations with two 'Scots kirks'. The Presbyterian Meeting House (1783, now demolished) was one, the 'Disruption' Presbyterian Church of 1848 the other, and this sponsored a school which moved to Osborne Road as Tweedmouth West Council School in 1906. Besides this, Tweedmouth National School (Tweedmouth East Council School) was established in 1824 and removed in 1868 to Mount Road.

The Tweed Dock at Tweedmouth was built 1872-77 by the Harbour Commissioners at a cost of £25,000 and was linked to Tweedmouth station by waterfront railway lines. These have been removed in the renovation of the waterfront, but one of the two shunting bridges remains. Along the waterfront too was built the Borough Waterworks on Dock Road in 1914.

Modern Tweedmouth is dominated by the East Coast railway embankment as it sweeps round to cross the Tweed and offers one of the most splendid railwayscapes in Europe. The western development of Tweedmouth is divided from the earlier manor by the embankment. Indeed Tweedmouth now extends to the west as far as the hamlet of East Ord and abuts the new A1 bypass. Across what is claimed to be the UK's longest and most complex steel-deck bridge, the long-planned Berwick bypass was completed in 1983 by Miller Construction in their £7.5 million contract for the 8.7km alternative route over the fast-flowing Tweed; this brought Berwick's bridges to four within the line of the old Liberties.

Tweedmouth Trading Estate was developed during the 1960s and 1970s and lies alongside the A698 to Coldstream and the west, across the road from the modern fire station. By the sixteenth century members of the Berwick Guild were expected to give service in fire fighting when needed; leather buckets were kept at the Tolbooth and every counciller had a bucket and overall.

Berwick Rangers Football Club is sited at Tweedmouth's Shielfield Park. The club was founded towards the end of 1881 and the players practised and played on various sites before Shielfield ground was established. The club was admitted into the Scottish league during the 1951/52 season. On 28 January 1967, Berwick Rangers FC had their moment of glory when they beat Glasgow Rangers, 1-0.

Tweedmouth and Spittal were formerly in North Durham, which was made up of those portions of the Bishopric of Durham which included Norhamshire, Islandshire and Bedlingtonshire, the most ancient of the See of Durham's properties, having been given by King Oswald to the church of Lindisfarne (*terra lindisfarnensis*). Norhamshire takes its name from 'Northern Home', and Norham Castle was built by the Prince-Bishop Ranulph Flambard. Islandshire was the easterly portion of North Durham.

Administratively Tweedmouth and Spittal formed areas of the old Borough of Berwick, and they had been parts of a medieval manor which was held in the socage (tenure of lands by service fixed and determined in quality) of the Bishop of Durham by such families as the Manners, Greys, Herons and Cheswicks; and the manor passed into lay hands on the dissolution of Durham Cathedral Priory in the sixteenth century. The area was always in some dispute in medieval times; for instance, in 1277 the Bishop of Durham complained that Alexander III of Scotland had made 'unwarranted encroachments' into Tweedmouth. In 1559 Bishop Tunstall of Durham refused to take the oath of allegiance to Queen Elizabeth and the temporalities of Tweedmouth were assumed by the Crown. Besides the archdeacon of the area, Tunstall had 'eyes and ears' hereabouts in the person of a suffragan bishop, one Thomas Sparke, erstwhile Prior of Lindisfarne, who took the title of Bishop of Berwick.

In 1657 the Corporation of Berwick purchased the Manor of

The *Shetland Trader* unloads at Tweedmouth Dock; the dock was built 1872-77 by the Harbour Commissioners at a cost of £25,000. In past days Tweedmouth had a great diversity of sailing vessels from fishing smacks to cargo sloops (*Neil Potts*).

Tweedmouth and Spittal for £570 from the parliamentarian-cum-courtier to Charles II, James Howard, 3rd Earl of Suffolk, and in 1835 the two were included in the Borough of Berwick by the Municipal Corporation Reform Act. The money for the purchase of the manors came out of the sequestered estates of the Jacobite Lord Mordington. From the seventeenth century a court was held at Tweedmouth during Easter and Michaelmas for the trial of debtors and trespassers.

Tweedmouth still retains its Feast which was originally held within the octave of St Boisil's Feast (February), but today it is held in July and is linked with the Crowning of the Salmon Queen. A special Feast Service is still held in St Bartholomew's church, and from 1988 the Tweedmouth Feast has been organised by the Tweedmouth Carnival & Crowning Commit-tee. In past years the Feast was a rumbustious affair with salmon boat races, wrestling matches, alfresco parties and a mock cere-mony to select 'the Mayor of Tweedmouth' who was ceremoni-ally ducked in the Tweed. The names of Muggers' (Tinkers')

Well and Beggar's Lane at Tweedmouth recall the earlier Feast.

The village of Tweedmouth appeared in one hereditary title. Dudley Coutts Majoribanks (1820-94: the surname is pronounced 'Marshbanks'), Liberal MP for Berwick (see page 184), was created Baron Tweedmouth of Edington in 1881. He was succeeded by his son Edward (1849-1909), also a Liberal MP (for Berwickshire) and his grandson Dudley Churchill Marjoribanks of Hutton Hall (1874-1935). The title became extinct on this grandson's death as his unmarried heir (his cousin Edward Marjoribanks) predeceased him in 1932.

CHAPTER 13

The Hamlet of Spittal

In the Middle Ages the wild, windswept roughlands on the southernmost shore of the mouth of the Tweed were known as the Manor of Spittal. Its earliest inhabitants, in their rough shiels (huts or sheds) of rubble and thatch, were fishermen and beachcombers and their superior was the Prince-Bishop of Durham. Nothing in modern Spittal is very old, and William Daniell's picture of Berwick and the mouth of the Tweed of 1822 shows the isolated and independent nature of Spittal which had lasted well into the nineteenth century. These days Spittal is reached from Berwick and Tweedmouth either along the south bank of the Tweed, via Dock View and Dock Road, or from the A1 (Northumberland Road) down Billendean Terrace and Billendean Road. From early inhabited times, however, there was a track along the Tweed which extended down the coast to Holy Island. The modern coastal path along the cliffs, south of Spittal, has the name 'Pilgrims' Way', and from medieval times this was an alternative route to the Great North Road taken mainly by pedlars, merchants and those having business between Holy Island and the churches of Berwick. Until the 1950s Spittal was reached by ferry across the Tweed from Berwick, and ferryboats like the *Susan* and the *Border Chief* were well-loved vessels.

Spittal owes its origin to fishing and its name to a hospital ('Spital' from *hospitium*). The modern Cul-de-sac of Hallowstell, above the old fishing beats at Spittal, recalls the 'holy man's fishing place' which was near the modern Stone Quay and was mentioned in a charter of the 1120s. The 'holy man' mentioned is thought to have been St Cuthbert, Bishop of Lindisfarne. Sandstell Road, along Spittal's north-western shore, marks out the second ancient 'fishing place on the sand'. This was the first inhabited area of Spittal and it still retains some of the old fishing shiels.

The lifeboat *Matthew Simpson* is paraded down Hide Hill, *circa* 1900, during a rainy gala day. The Royal National Lifeboat Institution was founded in 1824 and Berwick has always played an important rôle in RNLI fundraising. Berwick's lifeboat station was situated during 1900 to 1919 at Berwick Quay, after which it was moved to Spittal where there had been a lifeboat station from 1835 (*The Estate of M.I. Johnston*).

Somewhere in the region of the crossroads made today by Princes Street, Dock Road, Sandstell Road and Main Street stood the medieval leper hospital dedicated to St Bartholomew,

Boston's Bay View Yard, Spittal, pictured here *circa* 1885, was famous for its herring curing for the UK and European markets. The scene shows the herring gutters with their 'swills' (baskets) and tubs of herring, preparing the fish for smoking and pickling watched by their fellow workers and members of the Boston family. The smoke houses and coopering yards brought much employment to Spittal folk right into the twentieth century (*The Estate of M.I. Johnston*).

the first-century Apostle and Martyr. Founded before 1234, the hospital cared for the sick and lepers and was fortified in 1369. Before 1535 it was annexed to the hospital dedicated to God and St Giles, at Kepier, Durham, which had been founded by Ranulph Flambard, Bishop of Durham, in 1112. Most leper hospitals—and Spittal was one of two hundred or so in medieval England—had a chapel, a graveyard, a resident administrator and a priest who enacted the special leper's rite, *De separatione leprosorum*, and conducted the Mass of St Lazarus (the beggar in the Gospel of Luke).

It is likely that the hospital at Spittal never had more than ten lepers at any one time, and probably no more than two or three after the fourteenth century when the disease was declining. Consequently care of the aged sick would ultimately be a part of its duties; and its ultimate care for the 'crypellis, lamyt, blynd and pouir' is given precedence in the *Accounts of the Collectors of the Thirds of Benefices, 1561-72*. Who founded the hospital of St Bartholomew at Spittal is not known, and it is probable that it was supported by alms and revenues from bequests and properties; indeed the lands of the hospital stretched from Spittal to the glebes of Tweedmouth Parish Church. Because of its dedication to St Bartholomew it is likely that the hospital was administered by the Augustinians, possibly from Kepier. Its siting would be deliberate, for in the thirteenth century it was far enough away from Berwick and Tweedmouth to fulfil the requirements of the decree of the Lateran Council, under Pope Alexander III in 1179, that a leper should not mix with others, or share a church, or be buried with them. The hospital graveyard would be somewhere in the region of modern Princes Street.

Fishing was to remain Spittal's sole source of income until the nineteenth century. The commercial developers of the salmon fishing hereabouts were Berwick's Old Shipping Co., founded in 1764. The company transported salmon, and other goods, produce and passengers to London in the swift Berwick clippers and smacks. The owners of the company were craftsmen coopers (makers of the fish barrels) and fishery proprietors. The descendant of the Old Shipping Co. is the Berwick Salmon Fisheries Public Limited Company located at the corner of Sandstell Road and Main Street, which displays the figurehead of the vessel the *Lovely Polly* on the wall. The Berwick Shipping Co. Ltd was incorporated in 1856 but when the railway network caused a decline in the shipping trade the company concentrated efforts on improving its salmon fisheries. Eventually the sailing vessels were sold and on 18 December 1872 the company was changed to the Berwick Salmon Fisheries Co.Ltd. On 22 December 1980 the company was the first in Great Britain to register as a 'PLC' when its present name was adopted. Today it is involved in the marketing of frozen foods, but salmon fishing and processing using the old skills is still a principal business. The legal netting season on the Tweed extends from 15 February to 14 September.

Spittal remained a bustling fishing village throughout the height of the herring trade during the nineteenth and early twentieth centuries. There was a steady trade with Europe, particularly Russia and Germany, and this brought a great deal of work for fisherfolk in herring gutting, pickling, smoking and coopering. One famous name in the Spittal fish-curing business was Boston Bros., founded by Councillor Robert Boston (d.1891) around 1844. They had extensive curing, smoking and kippering sheds near the mouth of the Tweed employing over a hundred men and women during the season.

The old hamlet of Spittal began to develop in the eighteenth century. In those days Spittal was known for its manufacture of 'blue' used in laundries. One prominent manufacturer was Davidson of Spittal whose Prussia, Mecklenburgh and Fig blues went nationwide; yellow ochre for paints and dyes was also his forte. As people moved to Spittal to work, organised religion followed them. St Paul's United Reformed Church of 1878, in Main Street, is the descendant of the original Presbyterian Congregation formed in 1745 whose church was built in 1752. Within the Victorian building is the bell which was tolled to guide fishing boats into safe haven during foggy weather. In his *History*, John Fuller tells us that eighteenth-century Spittal's houses were 'intolerably bad' and not a good place to house 'the great number of people who resort to it in summer for the mineral water'. The Spa Well at Spittal (as an alternative to the Cat Well, Hide Hill, Berwick) was developed in the eighteenth century. Two wells remain (behind the Spittal War Memorial, Main Street), of which one has been dry for many years.

Spittal still retains a memory of the aftermath of the Jacobite rebellions. The Boundary Stones in North Greenwich Road (1885) still mark the limits of the Greenwich Hospital Estates in the hamlet. The old royal palace at Greenwich had been gifted by Queen Mary in 1692 to provide a Royal Naval Hospital for disabled seamen, and this hospital benefited from the forfeited properties of James Radcliffe, 3rd Earl of Derwentwater, executed at Tower Hill for his part in the Jacobite rebellion of 1716. Radcliffe had much property in Northumberland and the Scremerston and Spittal estates were to benefit the Greenwich Hospital.

The first quarter of the nineteenth century saw much activity in Spittal with the construction of Berwick Pier, 1810-21. From the old Ferryboat Landing area a railway ran down Main Street and South Greenwich Road to the stone quarries beyond Hud's Head. Waggons full of stone and pulled by horses were trundled to the stone quay; the waggons also descended the cliffs by gravity. This railway and the Carr Rock quay were also used later to transport the 'Greenwich Hospital Coals' from Scremerston colliery. The relics of the stationary winding gear can still be seen on the 'banks', with the line of the old railway, to the south of Spittal's promenade. On the cliffs here, above Hud's Head, by the old fishing shiel is the 'TOPP YE KNOWE STONE', the boundary stone of the old Manor of Spittal.

The old Admiralty Chart of Spittal for 1831 shows only two large houses, Roxburgh House and Seafield House, in Main Street. Seafield House was a bathing establishment in the 1820s and Roxburgh is the name of a modern licensed guest house. At this chart date (1831) there is no Billendean Road or Dock Road, only Main Street, West Street and Middle Street. And by 1847 Spittal was still a rather shabby place with an even shabbier people, it appears. Writing in 1847, the Rev William Whitehouse (c.1780-1857) of the Secession Church at Spittal writes: 'We have a greater proportion than I have seen or heard of in any village, of very aged, infirm, lame, maimed, drunken, dissolute and very poor persons. This is occasioned by the consequence of former smuggling practices, the Sabbath desecrations of the pilots and their families, the bondage system of the neighbouring monstrous large farms . . . .whose labourers when aged are not allowed a habitation on the lands on which were spent their strength and sweat, and they come here to occupy our many miserable hovels, to enjoy their starvation parish allowance; the disasters on the seas, and the

Spittal Main Street, with the parish church of St John the Evangelist on the right. The church was first licensed for divine service in 1867 and consecrated in 1871; the building was completed in 1894 when the tower was erected. Nearby Spittal School was built in 1908. The old light railway used to run down Main Street from the quarries at the south to the landing stage on Tweed shore (*Neil Potts*).

neighbouring collieries, producing many poor widows and orphans . . . . . Almost all young females and youths leave us for domestic service and employment in distant parts, or on the devouring sea . . . . . The railroad workers are also occasioning much evil amongst us by their profanity and drunkenness on the Sabbaths, and by their requiring the women at whose houses they are lodged to stay at home cooking for them . . . . . Spittal was, within these five years, insulated from Berwick, by the bad footways, and the tides when full preventing persons going the shortest way without climbing a dangerous rock . . . . . Now the rock is cut away, and the Spittal people and Summer bathers can walk dryshod . . . or have a pleasant ride for a penny in the . . . two steamers that ply between the village and Berwick'.

Following the wreck of the vessel *Christiana*, out of Stockholm, in November 1834, off Berwick with the loss of eight lives, there was an outcry for the provision of a lifeboat, and a public subscription list was drawn up. A 26ft lifeboat was stationed at Spittal from February 1835 and a boathouse was built in 1859. The lifeboat was stationed at Berwick Quay from 1900 to 1919 when it returned to Spittal and a new boathouse was built at Sandstell in 1929 from legacy monies of Mrs Maria Amelia Jeannopulos, and was resited at Carr Rock in 1939. The offshire lifeboat was withdrawn in 1976.

The Victorian and Edwardian eras saw the development of Spittal as a seaside resort. In those days whole families, accompanied by housemaids and valets, would take up residence every year for the summer season. They took up lodgings in rented accommodation, and in such hostelries as Mrs Thompson's Commercial Inn, or Mrs Geggie's digs at 34 Main Street. Most folk indulged in the Sea Water Baths run by A.C.Burn. Spittal was a favourite location for Sunday school outings, and from the 1880s such organisations as the Gala (Galashiels) Cycling Club held their annual 'camps' at Spittal, which was also on the booking circuit of the Pierrot Shows.

Of Spittal's main public buildings, St John the Evangelist Anglican Parish Church, Main Street may be mentioned. It was licensed for worship in 1867 and consecrated in 1871; the church building was completed in 1894 by the addition of the tower; the Anglican community had formerly been a part of the parish of Tweedmouth. A Congregational Church was opened at Spittal in 1887. Spittal British School (pre-1837) in School Lane, and Spittal National School (1872) in North Greenwich Road, were amalgamated into Spittal School in 1908. The Council School of Spittal Hall was erected in 1885 by the Pilot Lodge of the Good Templars. Today Spittal retains a number of original fishing houses and nineteenth-century villas of which good examples are the Manse (1869) facing the Vicarage (formerly Brighton House, 1830-50) at 129 Main Street and the fine porticoed villa, topped with busts, at 178 Main Street.

Spittal developed gas and chemical plants, and iron and spade works (now a printing works in Main Street), but the vestiges of these enterprises are being swept away from Spittal

Point. Spittal lost its industrial emphasis when the Tweedmouth Trading Estate was developed in the 1960s as firms moved away, and latterly it reverted to its former speciality of fishing. From early Spring to September the blue-painted salmon fishing boats were as common a sight on the Tweed, as were the cobbles of the twelfth-century fishermen.

CHAPTER 14

Berwick's Banks and Banking

The history of banking in Berwick is as complicated a piece of research as any medieval study. Today there are four banking companies in Berwick—the Royal Bank of Scotland plc, the Bank of Scotland, TSB England & Wales plc, and Barclays Bank plc—and all have their origins in the Berwick of the late eighteenth and early nineteenth centuries.

The British Linen Bank was incorporated in 1746 under the title of the British Linen Co. and opened its branch at Berwick in 1778. The company records show that the decision to open a branch in Berwick was due to increased business amongst the local merchants in the early 1770s. It was largely at the request of two Berwick merchants, Samuel Burn and James Craig, that the bank agreed to be represented. James Bell, a Berwick merchant and mayor of the town, acted as their first agent and through his influence the company increased business; Bell was particularly successful in processing the pay for the Durham Militia and the Cumberland Militia. When he died in 1817 the branch was closed as agricultural trade and the military presence were declining. The British Linen Bank reopened for trade in 1827.

During the latter part of the eighteenth century, the Dundee Bank (1763) and others used Berwick smacks to transport their gold from London. But after 1789 the dangers of privateering increased down the east coast and the specie was now conveyed to Scotland, via Berwick, by slow, heavy waggon.

In 1803 the Bank of Newcastle failed and its Berwick branch was closed, but local interests established a Berwick Bank which seems to have lasted until 1820.

In 1808 the Berwick and Kelso Banking Co. opened an office at Berwick and traded as the Tweed Bank until 1810. It is interesting to note that the firm of William Batson, Berry, John Langhorn and John Wilson also traded as the Tweed Bank and they went bankrupt in 1840 and completely ceased business in 1841. It seems that this was the only 'bank' to issue what might be called 'Berwick Banknotes'. Notes with their company's name and bearing an engraving of Berwick's old bridge are extant and most bear the frank marks of dividends paid to creditors.

The Berwick and Tweedmouth Savings Bank was formed on 13 February 1816 at a meeting held at Berwick Town Hall presided over by the mayor. On 19 February banking started in a room within the Dispensary House at Quay Walls and the new bank's rules provided for receipt of savings of 'Mechanics, Labourers, Servants and the Industrial Classes living in the Parishes of Berwick and Tweedmouth, and any other place not exceeding the distance of twenty miles . . . . . ' The first day's deposits were £26.1s.6d. From time to time the proximity of the bank to the Dispensary House caused alarm as cholera and other infectious diseases were treated just across the passage from the bank's office. But it was not until 1859 that the bank moved to the new Corn Exchange in Sandgate. There they stayed until 1884 when the British Linen Co. bought land in what was then known as Waugh Square; the Trustees of the Berwick and Tweedmouth Savings Bank now acquired a strip of land alongside the British Linen Co.'s building and engaged the Edinburgh architects Kinnear and Peddie to draw up plans for a new office. The Savings Bank moved into their new office in 1886 (it is now occupied by the Bank of Scotland). The bank suffered greatly in the economic upset caused by World War I and it was recommended that it be amalgamated with the Savings Bank of Newcastle; this was resisted but an amalgamation was effected on 21 November 1927. The Savings Bank continued to expand and is now located at 47 Hide Hill, occupying premises which formerly belonged to Martin's Bank; the Berwick and Tweedmouth Savings bank is now a part of TSB England and Wales plc.

The National Bank of Scotland (1825) had a presence in Berwick, as had the Commercial Bank from 1865. They joined up in 1910 and with Lloyds Bank in 1918 and amalgamated fully as the National Commercial Bank of Scotland in 1959. The Royal Bank of Scotland started a branch in Berwick in 1928 and the National Commercial merged with them in 1969.

By the 1840s the Northumberland and Durham Bank had a district office at 9-11 Bridge Street.

A Berwick branch of the Newcastle Shields and Sunderland Union Joint Stock Bank, NSS Bank for short, was opened in November 1848, although the first volume of the *Bankers' Almanack* (1845) notes that the NSS Bank had an agency in Berwick by the date of the book's publication. This bank owed its origins to the private firm of Chapman & Co., the Quaker financiers who established this company in 1818. It is clear too that this firm had agents in Berwick by 1820. The NSS Bank prospered but by the 1850s the joint stock banks in the north of England fell into disfavour and the NSS Bank was bought by Woods, Parker & Co. in 1859. Messrs Barclay & Co. Ltd bought Woods & Co. in 1897 and this was the first bank to be absorbed by Barclays since its formation in the eighteenth century. Barclay & Co. opened an office at the Corn Exchange, Sandgate, in 1905, subordinate to the already existing branch, and this sub-branch was closed in July 1968. Today Barclays Bank plc is located at 22/24 Hide Hill in an eighteenth-century building restored in 1973-74. The building was an earlier office of the Tweed Bank which had ceased trading by 1841.

By 1865 the Alnwick and County Bank (founded in 1858) had established an office in Berwick. This bank amalgamated with the North Eastern Banking Co. Ltd in 1875 which had itself been established at Newcastle, and acquired the former's branch at Berwick. This branch was not profitable and the managing director, Benjamin Noble, even ordered the local manager to stop buying the *Scotsman* newspaper in an attempt to save money. In 1914 the North Eastern Bank merged with the Bank of Liverpool and Martins Ltd (shortened to Martins in 1928) and in 1969 this bank merged with Barclays. At this time the old Martin's branch at 47 Hide Hill remained in business but under the control of the parent across the road, and on 23 February 1970 the branch was closed and the premises were sold to the Northumberland and Durham Savings Bank (TSB). The Bank of Liverpool and Martins Ltd, of course, had established a sub-office in addition to their Berwick branch at the Corn Exchange in July 1922, and this office was closed at the time of the 1969 merger.

The Bank of Scotland opened a sub-branch at Berwick in 1919 and it retained this status until 1964 when it became a full branch. It was managed from Coldstream as the Berwick business was not great. The branches of the British Linen Bank and the Bank of Scotland were merged shortly after the amalgamation of the companies in 1971.

CHAPTER 15

Members of Parliament for Berwick

The parliament of Henry III of 28 October 1258 was the first to which knights were sent from Northumberland; they were Sir Peter Cambo of Cambo, Sir John son of Simon of Mitford, Sir John Plessy of Plessy near Stannington, and Sir Thomas Fenwick of Fenwick. The role of these knights, who were not elected for Northumberland but selected by the sheriff, was 'to enquire . . . . touching certain trespasses and to bring their inquisitions personally to London'. After the Battle of Lewes, a parliament was held on 24 June 1264 and this was the first to which Northumbrian knights were elected to represent the county, but their names are not known. Records are sketchy regarding Northumbrian parliamentary representation during the Middle Ages, and the wars with Scotland made representation difficult. Known knights sent to parliament who had connections with Berwick's story during the thirteenth and fourteenth-centuries were few, but included Sir Adam of Swynburn, imprisoned at Berwick in 1297 for leading a Scots raid to burn Hexham, and Sir William Ridell of Tillmouth who served in the Berwick garrison in 1318.

Data on the early Members of Parliament for Berwick are very sparse, but it is known that from the 21st parliament of the reign of Henry VIII, the town sent two MPs. It was the general practice for the MPs for Berwick to be elected burgesses of the town, and generally the early candidates were members of the Merchant Guild who had been mayors and aldermen. Wealth, property ownership and clout were the main factors in MP selection. As the choice of candidate widened, representatives were chosen from such influential families of the neighbourhood as the Blakes, the Collingwoods, the Fenwicks, the Greys, the Ordes and the Selbys. In the eighteenth century the town was represented by members of the English, Scottish and Irish peerage, chosen rather for their influence than their popularity.

178

The sequence of MPs from 1529 to 1831 is compiled from the *known* returns made and there are date gaps in the records. The dates shown are when Parliament was summoned.

4th November 1529. Johannes Martyn.

Johannes Couper.

Nothing is known about these men and there were no further known returns until:

2nd April 1554

George Browne, burgess; mayor, 1547 and 1553.

Odonel Selby of Tweedmouth, burgess; mayor, 1536, 1540, 1551.

21st October 1555

Thomas Bradforthe. Died 1571. Burgess. Mayor five times between 1557-1569.

Thomas Wharton.

11th January 1563. Anthony Temple. Freeman, alderman, mayor 1562,1565,1571.

Thomas Norton. Executed at Tyburn 27 May 1570 for taking part in the Rebellion of the North, in which the Roman Catholic northern earls rebelled against Elizabeth I.

8th May 1572. Martin Garnet of Buckton Tower, Kyloe. Bailiff 1568-69, freeman from 1570. Corn merchant and dealer in salmon. Mayor 1577,1580. Known as 'a turbulent and factious' citizen often in dispute with his fellow burgesses.

Robert Newdigate. Died 1695.

23rd November 1584. William Morton. Alderman. Freeman. Mayor 1574, 1581, 1585, 1588.

Thomas Parkinson. Freeman, alderman,. Mayor eleven times between 1583 and 1618. A wealthy burgess. Between 1603-04 he was sent to London to procure the new charter from James VI & I. Died *circa* 1619.

15th October 1586. Sir Valentine Browne. Before 1576 treasurer and Queen's victualler at Berwick. Freeman and alderman.

Thomas Parkinson.

12th November 1588. William Morton.

(Sir) William Selby of Twizell, Gentleman-Porter. Left property in his will to found a free grammar school in Berwick. Died 1612.

19th February 1593. William Morton.

(Sir) William Selby Jr. Burgess. Gentleman-Porter.

MP 1593-97. d.1637.

24th October 1597. Sir William Selby.

Thomas Parkinson.

27th October 1601. Sir William Selby, Sr.

David Waterhouse of Halifax. Barrister of the Middle Temple.

19th March 1604. Sir William Selby.

Christopher Parkinson, Recorder of Berwick.

5th April 1614. Sir George Selby. Elected, but as Sheriff of Durham he was ineligible to sit as an MP.

Sir William Selby Jr replaced Sir George.

(Sir) Robert Jackson. Freeman 1595. Alderman. Bailiff 1596. Collector of Customs. Mayor five times between 1605 and 1640. Wealthy merchant of Berwick; negotiated money for the building of Berwick Bridge.

16th January 1621. Sir Robert Jackson.

Sir John Selby of Twizell. d.1636.

12th February 1624. Sir Robert Jackson.

Edward Lyvely. Probably Constable of Durham Castle 1617-28.

27th March 1625. Sir John Selby.

Sir Robert Jackson.

6th February 1626. Sir Robert Jackson.

Richard Lowther. Free burgess. Queen's Commissioner.

17th March 1628. Edward Lyvely.

Sir Edward Sawyer. Auditor of the Court of Exchequer. Owner of fisheries in Berwick. Disabled from being an MP in 1628, having tampered with witnesses in a law case. He was replaced by Sir Robert Jackson.

13th April 1640. This parliament was summoned on the advice of Thomas Wentworth, 1st Earl of Strafford (1593-1641), to obtain supplies for waging the second Bishops' War. Charles I offered to give up Ship Money (a tax on shipping to be used to protect vessels against piratical attacks) in return for subsidies but the MPs insisted that he redress grievances in church and state as a first condition. Learning that the MPs were about to petition against the Scottish war, Charles dissolved parliament, 5th May 1640. Known as the Short Parliament.

Sir Thomas Widdrington. MP for Northumberland in 1656.

Hugh Potter. Royalist. Principal agent for the Earl of Northumberland. d.1661.

3rd November 1640. Long Parliament. Summoned after Charles I's defeat in the second Bishops' War. Ran on until 16th March 1660.

Sir Thomas Widdrington.

Lt. General Sir Edward Osborne. 1596-1647. Vice-President of the Council of the North which dealt with special problems in the Borders. He resigned as MP in 1640 and was replaced by Robert Scawin, agent for the Duke of Northumberland.

22nd January 1644. Anti Parliament at Oxford.

7th Feb 1649. Interregnum.

16th December 1653. Oliver Cromwell Lord Protector.

During the period 1644-53 no members represented Berwick.

3rd September 1654. Col. George Fenwick of Brinkburn. 1603-57. Governor of Berwick, 1649.

17th September 1656. Col. George Fenwick.

John Rushworth. 1612-90. Barrister, Secretary to Cromwell. MP 1657-81. Recorder of Berwick.

3rd September 1658. Richard Cromwell, Lord Protector.

No members.

27th January 1659. John Rushworth.

George Paylor. Treasurer of Berwick garrison, 1648.

25th April 1660. Convention Parliament called after the final dissolution of the Long Parliament. Effected the Restoration of Charles II.

Sir Thomas Widdrington.

John Rushworth.

Col. Edward Grey. Replaced Sir Thomas Widdrington in 1660. Royalist and lawyer. Died *circa* 1676.

8th May 1661. Pensionary Parliament, also called Cavalier Parliament, 1661-79. Royalist majority. Took the name 'pensionary' from the acceptance of bribes by its members. It was notable for the growth of 'party politics' and it extended the control by parliament of domestic and foreign issues.

Sir Thomas Widdrington.

Col. Edward Grey.

(Lt.Col.) Daniel Collingwood. Replaced Sir Thomas Widdrington in 1665. Lawyer. Governor of Holy Island, 1672. Tory. Died 1681.

Peregrine Osborne, Viscount Dunblane. Replaced Col.Edward Grey in 1677. MP for Berwick 1677-79. Became Vice-Admiral of the Red, 1703. Succeeded as 2nd Duke of Leeds. Died 1729.

6th March 1679-21st March 1681.

John Rushworth.

Ralph Grey of Wark. Whig. MP 1679-81; 1695-1701. Became Governor of Barbados, 1698-1701. Died 1706.

6th February 1685. Philip Bickerstaffe, MP for Northumberland 1689.

Ralph Widdrington. Lawyer. Died 1718. He was blinded in the Dutch Wars of William III.

22nd January 1689. Convention Parliament authorised by William of Orange. It declared the throne vacant and offered it to William and Mary together.

Francis Blake of Ford Castle. MP for Northumberland 1701.

Col. Philip Babington. Lawyer. Governor of Berwick 1688-89. Died *circa* 1690.

20th March 1690. Sir Francis Blake of Ford Castle.

Samuel Ogle of Bowsden. Lawyer. Recorder of Berwick 1689-98.

22nd November 1695-6th February 1701.

Ralph Grey.

Samuel Ogle.

Jonathan Hutchinson. Replaced Sir Francis Blake in 1702. Merchant. Died 1711.

20th August 1702-8th July 1708.

Samuel Ogle.

Jonathan Hutchinson.

25th November 1710. Jonathan Hutchinson.

Col. William Kerr. Fought at the Battle of Sheriffmuir, 13th November 1715. Courtier to George, Prince of Wales, 1714. MP for Berwick 1710-23. Died 1741.

Richard Hampden. Replaced Jonathan Hutchinson in 1711. Treasurer of the Navy, 1717-20. Great-grandson of John Hampden (1594-1643), English parliamentarian and civil war leader. Died 1728.

12th November 1713. Richard Hampden.

William Orde of Berwick. Died 1748.

17th March 1715. Grey Neville (1681-1723). MP for Berwick 1715-22. Walpolian Whig.

John Barrington (*alias* Shute). Barrister. MP for Berwick 1715-22. Expelled from parliament for fraudulent dealing. Born in 1678, he became Viscount Barrington of Ardglass, Ireland, in 1720 and died in 1734.

10th May 1722. Grey Neville.

John Barrington.

Henry Grey. Replaced John Barrington in 1723. Lawyer. Sheriff for Northumberland 1735-37. Died 1749.

William Kerr. Replaced Grey Neville in 1723.

28th November 1727. George Liddell (1678-1740).

General Joseph Sabin (*circa* 1662-1739).

13th June 1734. George Liddell.

Hugh Home (1708-94; later Lord Polwarth). Anti-Walpole Tory. Keeper of the Great Seal, 1764-94.

William Wildman Barrington-Shute (1717-93) Replaced Lord Polwarth 1740. MP for Berwick 1740-54. High offices included Chancellor of the Exchequer 1751-62.

Deputy Commissioner Thomas Watson (1701-66). Replaced George Liddell in 1740. Burgess and Mayor of Berwick six times from 1727 to 1739.

25th June 1741-13th August 1747.

William, Viscount Barrington.

Thomas Watson.

31st May 1754. Thomas Watson.

(Sir) John Hussey Delaval of Ford Castle (1728-1808).

Tory MP for Berwick 1754-86. (This was the colourful contest when the radical Whig, John Wilkes, appeared against Delaval.)

19th May 1761. Thomas Watson.

(Col.) John Craufurd. Died in 1765 when commandant at Menorca.

Sir John Hussey Delaval, replaced John Craufurd in 1765.

Wilmot Vaughan, created Earl of Lisburn in 1776. Replaced Thomas Watson in 1766. Died 1800.

10th May 1768. Sir John Hussey Delaval.

Robert Paris Taylor. Died 1792 in the Fleet Prison as debtor.

29th November 1774. Jacob Wilkinson. Died 1791 aged 74.

(Lt.Gen.) John Vaughan. Governor of Berwick. Died 1795.

31st October 1780. Maj.Gen. John Vaughan.

Sir John Hussey Delaval.

1st May 1784. Lt.Gen. John Vaughan.

Baron Delaval.

Sir Gilbert Elliot (1751-1814) replaced Baron Delval in 1786. MP for Berwick 1786-90. Governor General of India 1806-13.

10th August 1790. Lt.Gen. John Vaughan.

Charles Carpenter (c.1757-1803).

Col. John Callendar (1739-1812), replaced John Vaughan in 1795. MP for Berwick 1795-1807.

12th July 1796. John Callendar.

George Carpenter, Earl of Tyrconnell in Ireland (1750-1805).
31st August 1802. Thomas Hall and John Fordyce were elected, but their election was declared void because of criminal proceedings. They were replaced by:
Francis Sitwell of Barmoor Castle. Died 1813.
Lt. Col. Alexander Allan, a Director of the Hon. East India Company. Died 1820.
13th December 1806. Sir John Callendar.
Lt. Col. Alexander Tower. Died 1813.
22nd June 1807. Lt. Col. Alexander Allan.
Col. Sir Alexander Macdonald Lockhart. Died 1816.
24th November 1812— 4th August 1818.
Lt. Col. Alexander Allan.
Lt. Col. Henry Heneage St Paul. Died 1820.
21st April 1820. Charles Augustus Bennet (1776-1859), called Lord Ossulston. Became Earl of Tankerville in 1822.
Admiral Sir David Milne (1763-1849). Election declared void, replaced by Lt. Col. Henry Heneage St Paul.
25th July 1826. General Marcus Beresford.
John Gladstone (father of the future Liberal Prime Minister, W.E. Gladstone). Election void.
Sir Francis Blake (c.1775-1860). Whig. MP for Berwick 1826-35.
14th September 1830— 14th June 1831.
Sir Francis Blake.
General Marcus Beresford.

Acts of Parliament were first printed in 1501; the first Parliament of Great Britain was held on 23rd October 1707; and the Act making it necessary to have General Elections every seven years was passed 7 May 1716. The first Parliament of the United Kingdom of Great Britain and Ireland was held in 1801. Under Edward I county MPs had been elected by Berwick's freeholders and from 1430 to 1832 by all freeholders of property valued at 40/- (£2) per annum. From the Reform Bill of 1832 the new franchise was based on the occupation of rateable property. By the Acts of 1832, 1867 and 1884 successive classes of the population were called to vote; by 1918 all males over 21 and all females over 30 were given the vote; and in 1929 females between 21 and 30 were enfranchised. Universal suffrage for all over 18 was established in 1970.

December 1832. Sir Francis Blake.
Col. Sir Rufane Shaw Donkin (1773-1841). Whig. Surveyor General of the Ordnance 1835.
1835. James Bradshaw. Conservative. Died 1847.

Col. Sir Rufane Shaw Donkın.

July/August 1837. Richard Hodgson of Carham Hall. Born 1812. Conservative. Chairman of the North British Railway Co. MP for Berwick 1837-47.

William Holmes (1779-1861).

June/July 1841. Richard Hodgson.

Matthew Forster. Liberal. MP for Berwick 1841-53.

July 1847. Matthew Forster.

John Campbell Renton, Mordington House. Conservative. Born 1814. MP for Berwick 1847-52.

July 1852—April 1853. Matthew Forster.

John Stapleton (1815-91). Barrister. Whig. In 1853 his election was declared void owing to bribery and treating the electors. MP for Berwick 1857-59, 1868-74.

Sir Dudley Coutts Majoribanks (1820-94). Banker. Liberal. MP 1853-Apr. 1859; Aug. 1859-Dec. 1868. Re-elected Feb. 1874-1881.

John Forster, born 1817, was first returned in May 1853 when his father Matthew Forster was unseated on petition. Defeated 1857.

April 1857. John Stapleton.

Sir Dudley Coutts Majoribanks.

May 1859. Captain C.W. Gordon. Conservative. MP 1859-63. Died in 1863 and was replaced by:

William Walter Cargilll (1813-94). Conservative. MP 1863-65.

Ralph Anstruther Earle (1835-79). Private Secretary to Rt.Hon. Benjamin Disraeli while Chancellor of the Exchequer in 1858. Conservative supporter of Lord Derby. Took the Chiltern Hundreds in August 1859.

Sir Dudley Coutts Majoribanks.

July 1865. Sir Dudley Coutts Majoribanks.

Alexander Mitchell (1831-73). Independent Liberal. MP until retirement in 1868.

November 1868. William Coutts Keppel, styled Viscount Bury (1832-94). Gladstonian Liberal. Retired 1874.

John Stapleton.

1879. Sir Dudley Coutts Majoribanks.

Captain David Milne Home of Paxton House. Born 1838. Conservative. MP for Berwick 1874-1880 and 1880-1885.

19th July 1880. Sir Dudley Coutts Majoribanks.

Hon. Henry Strutt (1840-1914). Liberal. Served Apr.-Jun. 1880 when he succeeded as Baron Belper, and was replaced by Capt. David Milne Home.

1881. This year marked the last election for Berwick as a separate borough, after sending two MPs (dubbed 'senior' and 'junior') to the English Parliament for almost 360 years.

Captain David Milne Home.

Sir Dudley Coutts Majoribanks. He was created Baron Tweedmouth in 1881 and was replaced by:

(Sir) Hubert Edward Henry Jerningham of Longridge Towers (1842-1914). He was a Gladstonian Liberal. Governor of Mauritius 1893-97, and

Trinidad 1897-1900.

7th July 1885. This date marked the redistribution of seats in which Berwick was merged into the Berwick Division of North Northumberland represented by one MP.

Sir Edward Grey (1862-1933), Home Rule Liberal. MP 1885-1916. Foreign Secretary 1905-16. With William Beveridge, Grey was one of the 'two political greats' who represented Berwick. The *Dictionary of National Biography* (1949) says: 'The mutual affection that grew up between the young member and the fishermen, shepherds and others . . . who supported him, was one of the chief things that kept him in political life'. He was created a peer as Viscount Grey of Fallodon and there was a bye-election on 17 August 1916.

1916-1922. Sir Francis Douglas Blake (1856-1940) of Tillmouth Park. Barrister. Liberal.

1922-1923. Hylton Philipson (1892-1941). National Liberal. Election declared void.

1923-1929. Mrs (Mabel) Hylton Philipson (1887-1951). Actress. Conservative. Elected in June 1923 in succession to her husband. Re-elected December 1923.

1929-1935. Col. Alfred John Kennett Todd (1890-1970). Captain in the Queens Bays. Tory Agent for Berwick. Elected May 1929. Returned unopposed October 1931. Defeated 1935.

1935-1941. Sir Hugh Michael Seely (1898-1970). Soldier and airman. Liberal PPS to the Rt. Hon. Sir Archibald Sinclair when he was Secretary of State for Air (1940-45). Created Baron Sherwood 1941.

Bye-election 18 August 1941.

Lt. George Charles Grey. Liberal. Born 1918, killed in action in 1944.

1944-1945. Sir William Henry Beveridge (1879-1963). Liberal. British social reformer and economist who drew up the Beveridge Plan (1942) which formed the basis for the present social security system. Defeated by the Tories and created a peer as Baron Beveridge. His biographer, José Harris (1977), described Berwick as 'a far-flung border constituency of sheep-farmers and small tradesmen, who had consistently voted Liberal throughout the Liberal twilight of the 1920s and 1930s'.

1945-1951. Brigadier Robert Allen Fenwick Thorp (1900-66). Conservative Whip 1947-48.

1951-1973. Anthony Claud Frederick, Viscount Lambton (b 1922). Disclaimed title 1970. Elected October 1951; Parliamentary Under-Secretary of State for Defence for the RAF 1970-73. Resigned after public concern over his casual acquaintance with a callgirl.

1973- Alan James Beith (b.1943). Won bye-election November 1973. Chief Whip of the Liberal Party 1976-86. Deputy Leader of the Liberal Party and Spokesman on Foreign Affairs 1985.

During the sixteenth century, it may be noted, Berwick's MPs were allowed 3s.4d. (16½p) per day, whereas today the MP's parliamentary salary is in excess of £18,500 plus expenses and allowances.

Today the whole of Alnwick District is within Berwick-upon-Tweed Constituency, as well as the fourteen parishes of Castle Morpeth Borough Council and the thirty-eight parishes of Berwick-upon-Tweed Borough Council.

CHAPTER 16

Food for the Mind: Education in Berwick

Both the *Kelso Chartulary* and the *Chronicle of Lanercost* tell us of the monastic schools in Berwick, but by the sixteenth century only one in three of Berwick's property owners and 'gentry' could be considered literate. Schoolmasters were being hired privately in Berwick in the reign of Edward VI, and in Mary Tudor's day one schoolmaster is recorded in the town at 50/- a quarter. By the early seventeenth century education in Berwick was linked to a practical purpose. The town's *Guild Book* records, for 6 September 1604, *inter alia*: 'John Wark is also admitted to the freedom of this town in regard of his great care he hath of bringing up young children and youth, in teaching them and setting them on work to knit and spin, and in regard hereof the Guild accept a small fine of the sum of £3. 6s. 8d for his admittance'.

Writing in his *Sketch of the History of the Berwick Grammar School* (1875), Robert Douglas, the then Town Clerk, noted: 'The first active step to found any school in Berwick took place in the year 1604. The Parish Church had been allowed to fall into such a state of disrepair that it was impossible to hold divine service in it, and the Guild (then composed of almost all the inhabitants, who took the entire charge of the ecclesiastical as well as civil interests of the town) being too poor to rebuild it, agreed to send the Mayor to London, at their expense, to solicit assistance from the Court for the purpose of building a new Church, and also founding a College, but there is no account of the result of the mission, and it was, apparently, not successful'. Even so, records show that the original idea of starting a Grammar School in Berwick was that of Sir William Selby MP (c.1532-1612), a town burgess himself; and it appears that a school of sorts was started. In 1577 there were three schools in Berwick and by 1603 there were two, run by Aristotle Knowsley and John Parke.

The site of the first Grammar School and master's dwelling house was to the south of Marygate and its policies extended from the main street to Bankhill; in the sixteenth century the land had belonged to Ralph Colvill of Tweedmouth and was eventually taken over by the Selby family. On Sir William Selby's death he bequeathed his Marygate property to the town. The fate of the school was uncertain for some time and up to 1620 there is some evidence that it did not function. There was, however, a temporary arrangement by which pupils were taught Latin; so by 1633 a Latin School was being run free for burgesses' children by one John Jackson. By 1645 an extensive subscription list was set up to give a permanent school a proper foundation. By 1646 the Puritan William Webb was in position as first master of the Grammar School, which was then sited at a house in the churchyard and moved around 1651 to the property bequeathed by Sir William Selby. The schoolroom was enlarged *circa* 1657. The site was always subject to some dispute with the Selby family.

The Grammar School survived the vicissitudes of the Parliamentarians and the Restoration, and by 1708 it needed enlarging. A new schoolhouse was built in 1754 on the site of what is now 101-109 of the upper corner of Marygate and Golden Square.

The Grammar School taught only classics and a broader-based education was required. The Guild determined to build their own Academy in 1798. It merged with a writing school which had been founded in the seventeenth century, and it may be noted that there were five schools in the town when the Academy was built. It was completed in 1800 and it was the school in which the children of the freemen of the town were educated until its close in 1921. A new Grammar School was begun on the adjacent site in 1819 and the premises were used until 1866 when the school was moved to Palace Street East and sited in an eighteenth-century building. There it remained until it moved to the Girls' High School (now Berwick Middle School, Northumberland Avenue) in 1939; the premises are now used as a Youth and Community Centre.

The Elementary Education Act was passed on 9 August 1870 and education was made compulsory in 1876 (it was not 'free' until 1891). By this date there were several private schools in the town as well as the following: The Boys' National School, Ravensdowne; it had begun as a Charity School in 1725 and in 1842 it was rebuilt and merged with the National system. The school was closed in 1932 when the pupils were moved to the Parade. The Girls' National School and the Infants' National School were to be found at the Parade. The British School for Boys and Girls, opened in 1859 at Palace Green, was for the education of Nonconformist children and it was closed in 1975. Today it is a boarding hostel for pupils (mainly from Holy Island) who attend Berwick Middle and High Schools. There was a Berwick Infants' School at College Place and St Mary's National School in Castlegate which was opened in 1866 and closed in 1972. The Bell Tower School was constructed as an Infants' School in 1903 and it became a senior school in 1932 and was formed into part of Berwick Middle School in 1976. Also part of the Middle School is the erstwhile Berwick Grammar School in Northumberland Avenue which was in the buildings originally set up in 1927 for the Berwick Girls' High School with which the old Boys' Grammar School was merged in 1939.

Another school which played a large part in the educational life and times of Berwick was St Mary's Convent School which was established in a villa in Tweed Street in 1889. Beginning as an elementary school, it expanded to take in Protestant girls as well as Roman Catholic on a fee-paying basis. The oratory of the convent was built in 1907 and its rose window is still to be seen, although the building is now the Tweed View Hotel. A prominent patron of the school was Sir Hubert Jerningham (1842-1914) of Longridge Towers, MP for Berwick 1881-1885, and it was to his former home that the convent and school removed in 1950. From 1889 until 1983 the school was run by the Ursuline Sisters of the Incarnation, and when the convent closed the property was sold to a Charitable Trust formed mainly by parents of the pupils of the school, and it still flourishes today. Longridge Towers had been built in 1878 by Sir Hubert, who lavished embellishments upon it in the fond hope that the future Edward VII would stay, but he was to be disappointed.

CHAPTER 17

Discovering Berwick's History

There is something faintly magical about the sound of the words 'The Great North Road'; magical enough for the phrase to be spelled in capitals when the touring company encountered the ancient way in J.B.Priestley's *The Good Companions* of 1929. It is a very long road, almost four hundred miles of it from London to Edinburgh, and as the northernmost town in England, Berwick-upon-Tweed sits on its tip as the road drives forth into Scotland. And though Berwick was bypassed in 1982-83 by the new concrete bridge and road across the Tweed that skirts the hamlet of East Ord, the town is given rank with York, Newcastle and London in historical importance, for it was the launching pad up the Great North Road for any discovery or subjugation of south-east Scotland. Indeed the miles to Berwick were long used as a colloquial distance proverb. For instance, Geoffrey Chaucer used it as such in *The Prologue to the Canterbury Tales* (Pardoner, 692): 'From Berwick to Ware'.

At Berwick the mail-coach travellers caught their breath at the posting-houses of the King's Arms, the Castle, Salmon, Hen and Chickens and the Red Lion, and for many it was their first flavour of Scottishness. Although firmly in England, Berwick still has a Scottish heart—its newspaper readers have a Scottish bias, its domestic menu has a Scottish flavour and its football team is in the Scottish League; and, sitting fifty-seven miles from Edinburgh (Newcastle-upon-Tyne is sixty-four miles to the south), it has a Scottish atmosphere.

Berwick's growth and prosperity arose largely from its advantageous location. It possessed a good natural harbour, suitable for both fishing and trading ships, and commanded the lowest point at which the river Tweed might be forded at low tide. Food supplies too were plentiful nearby, for fish was

191

obtainable from both river and sea and the land is rich. Salmon in particular formed part of the staple trade of the town, and along with wool and hides was a considerable source of wealth to the burgesses. Up to the mid-eighteenth century salmon was salted and pickled in Berwick for export to the Continent and shipment to the south. In 1788 it was discovered that by packing salmon in ice it was possible to keep it long enough to survive transportation without boiling; hence the decline of the boiling trade in Berwick, but Berwick salmon has kept its reputation and is transported still.

The borough's acres, name and status

Berwick, with the neighbouring hamlets of Tweedmouth and Spittal on the south side of the River Tweed, formed the Borough of Berwick-upon-Tweed until 1974. Then an enlarged District Council, with the same name, was established. The modern boundaries of the Borough of Berwick-upon-Tweed take in the established 'liberties' to the north of the Tweed (see page 72), and from just north of the Union Chain Bridge the boundary (and Scottish Border) follow the Tweed to just west of the village of Carham; it then meanders south to The Schil (1985 ft), and skirts south of Cheviot (2674ft) and Hedgehope Hill (2343 ft) to arc around Ingram, crossing the A697 north of Powburn. Thence the boundary cuts across the A1 to the North Sea, just south of Beadnell.

Historians put forward three theories as to the origin of Berwick's name. If Berwick is made up of the Anglo-Saxon *bere* and *wic,* it has a literal meaning of 'barley farm'. But if *berewic* is given the alternative meaning of a unit of a larger manorial estate, it may have been part of a now vanished Saxon messuage dating from the founding of the Kingdom of Northumbria and was maybe the fief of a supporter of King Ina (d.560). Others give Berwick a pure Norse origin, and all are likely to be conjointly correct.

The standard spelling of Berewic as *Berewich* seems to have become the norm in the *Exchequer Pipe Rolls* by 1194. The tradition

The removal of Berwick Borough Museum and Art Gallery to the old 'Clock Block' of Berwick Barracks was a happy circumstance. The museum reflects the town, Guild and borough history and houses treasures from the Sir William Burrell collection of pictures and decorative art. The museum is also a centre of ongoing historical research with regular programmes of thematic displays. The 'Clock Block' was built around 1746 and was used as a store and magazine (*Neil Potts*).

of calling the town Berwick-*upon*-Tweed is at least as old as the thirteenth century. In the Close Rolls for 1229 it appears as *Berewicum super Twedam* and in the *Staffordshire Court Roll* for 1599, in a mention of one George Holmer, a supervisor of the Berwick tournaments, it is referred to as *Berwicke super Twyde*. In several manuscripts before 1850 the town is referred to as 'The good town o' Berwick', and in Victorian times the town was noted in official documents as 'Her Majesty's Good Town of Berwick-upon-Tweed'. One eighteenth-century gazetteer offers this as a description: 'The Utmost Towne of England seated between two mighty kingdoms, shooting into the sea'. The River Tweed is first mentioned by Bede, c. 730, as *Tuidi fluminis*.

Because of its importance and the peculiarities of its position,

H

Berwick was mentioned, up to 1746, as a separate entity in Acts of Parliament; even later it was mentioned specifically in some official documents. This gives rise to the erroneous story that Berwick is still at war with Imperial Russia. The story goes that the declaration of war with Russia in 1854 included Berwick's name separately; but when the Treaty of Paris was drawn up at the end of the Crimean War in 1856 Berwick's name was omitted. It is a tale beloved of international journalists and tap-room historians.

Even with the local government reorganisation of 1974, Berwick is still 'out on a limb' with its own distinctive character. Unlike York, for instance, Berwick was not expanded by the coming of the railway. Yet despite its traditional isolation Berwick remains a lively meeting place for the folks who live within a twenty-five mile radius. And it retains its atmosphere by being a 'free town'—for long centuries it existed as a town not belonging in or to either England or Scotland, or to any country, being a county in itself. And it was good that when Berwick was granted modern borough status by royal charter the offices of mayor and sheriff were retained, Berwick's traditions and civic ceremonies remaining also.

Rhymes, sayings, dialect and taboo language in Berwick

Berwick appears in a number of rhymes and folk sayings of which one, 'Berwick, the Key of England on the East Sea', is typical. The dramatist and song-writer Charles Dibden (1745-1814) refers to Scotland's keys in *Observation on a Tour* (1801-02): 'The governor of Berwick Castle, in the 13th, 14th & 15th centuries, might be said to wear the Keys of Scotland in his Girdle'.

In James Johnston's (1750-1811) *Scots Musical Museum* there is a portion of a song, 'Go to Berwick Johnny', which purports to date from the later fourteenth century:

> Go to Berwick Johnny,
> Bring her frae the Border;
> We'll cry 'Fye upon ye',

If ye let her further.
The English loons will twyne
Ye, of your winsome treasure;
And ere ye so her tyne,
Your sword wi' them I'd measure.
Go to Berwick Johnny,
And redeem your honour;
Before the sun rise on ye,
Shew our Scottish banner.
I am Rab the king,
And ye are Jock my brither;
Or, we brook sic thing,
We'se a' be there thegither.
Go to Berwick Johnny,
On yer braid sword bind ye;
Wi' a' my graith upon me,
I'll be close behind ye,
Ye'll ride on the colt,
And I'll ride on the filly;
Saddle horse and mare,
And we'll to Berwick, billy!

M.A.Denham of Piersbridge, Darlington, writing in 1846-49, quotes in his *Folk-Lore* an odd verse of a 'good old Border Song', similar to the last verse of 'Berwick Johnny' which he gathered for *Northern Nursery Lore*:

Ride away! Ride away!
Ride away to Berwick Johnny:
Ye'll ride on the Brown Colt,
And I'll ride on the Filly.

Dr John Fuller noted a distinctive Berwick sound, which he called a 'wharring' in the throats of Berwick people 'so that they cannot pronounce the letter R'; such a sound became known as 'the Berwick Burr' and gave a distinctiveness to local spoken English and local dialect.

In terms of dialect Berwick had four main speech territories: Berwick proper; the Greenses'; Tweedmouth; and Spittal. Dialect researchers in Victorian times identified the Berwick patois as being 'a bastard Hindustani' and likened it to the 'language' spoken by such as 'the muggers o' Yetholm'.

Indeed while Berwick's predominant accent was 'Northumbrian', with 'Scottish Lowland' second, the prevalent influence on Berwick dialect as spoken by the working classes was the language of the 'muggers'. The 'muggers' were the local gypsies who were established in the region by 1500 or so, and were driven by the contemporary draconian laws to the then remote places like Kirk Yetholm, whence they could disappear into the Cheviot Hills if hunted by law officers. In the eighteenth century the Bennets of Grubet, who owned Kirk Yetholm, built cottages for them, and from this important gypsy centre the muggers hawked their wares as far as Berwick and beyond. Several of Berwick's Victorian working-class families were descended from the muggers. Based on the vocabulary of the muggers, this then is a sampling of the Berwick working class vocabulary:

Barri—Big	Line—Thrash
Bing—Devil	Manishi—Woman
Chavi—Child	Mar—Hit, or punish
Churi—Knife	Mort—Woman
Chutli—Pipe (for tobacco)	Nash—Flee
Clemi—Stone	Pani—Water
Deek—See	Shan—Poor quality
Gadgi—Man	Swushy—Hare
Gri—Horse	Wing—Penny
Guffi—Pig	Yagi—Randy (also a fire)
Horni—Policeman	Yak—Eye
Jan—Look	Yarri—Egg
Juggal—Dog	Yukki—Stone
Keir—House	Cuffi/Radge/Steen—stupid

So a phrase might be rendered: *Deek thon gadgi wi' the barri sneck an' the juggal* (See that man with the large nose and the dog).

The words may be compared with the muggers' vocabulary collected by the Rev.John Baird, minister of Kirk Yetholm, in his *Memoir* (1862). Although still known, but rarely used today in Berwick, the vocabulary had its heyday in mid-Victorian times and was fading fast by the 1920s. Despite the Victorian local cliché of its association with Hindustani, it is more than unlikely that the words were related to any Indian language.

Berwick's fisherfolk were amongst the most superstitious in

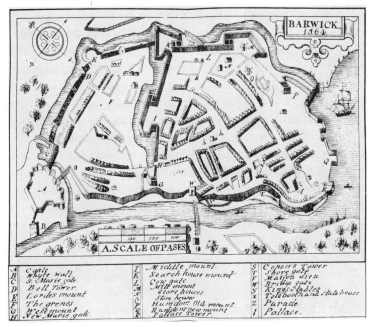

W.H. Lizars' print of the map of 'Barwick 1564' based on the plans of
Rowland Johnson, the Surveyor of Works at Berwick. The position of
the medieval tolbooth (the precursor of the Town Hall of 1750-61) is
set in 'New Marie gate' with the town crosses. This is a useful map to
compare and contrast with the following to show the surviving pattern
of Berwick's medieval streets.

Great Britain and they added several taboo words to the
folklore vocabulary of the nation. Berwick seamen and
fishermen and their families avoided the word 'cat' at sea, but to
have a cat aboard ship was deemed lucky. Cats were adept at
saving themselves from a sinking ship and were thought to be
equally powerful as good luck omens or bringers of good
fortune. The word 'dog' too should not be spoken at sea, the old
folk said, and few Berwick seamen would take a dog aboard ship
because they brought bad luck if they howled near the vessel.

'Drowning' was a word never to be uttered on board, for
obvious reasons, but the eschewing of the word 'eggs' has a

more arcane origin. It was a common superstition that eggs
were used by witches to transport themselves across water,
hence fisher children were taught to break a hole in the bottom
of their egg when they had finished; so, sailors and fishermen
used the word 'roundabout' instead of egg. Other words to
avoid were 'hare' and 'rabbit', both long associated with
witches as familiars and animals into which they transformed
themselves, and Berwick fishermen were known to turn back
after seeing a hare or rabbit on the way to the boats. The word
'pig' when uttered was deemed enough to raise a storm, but
fisherwomen of Berwick, Tweedmouth and Spittal, the *Denham
Tracts* tell us, when making black or white puddings, silently
dedicated each tying knot to some absent seaman, as the
pudding was flung into the pot. Again, Berwick fisherfolk
thought it bad luck to change a vessel's name.

To counter a taboo word blurted out by mistake the
transgressor could 'touch wood'—an appeal to the protection
of the True Cross—or 'touch iron', the latter being long
invested with magical properties usually in the form of the great
superstition protect-all of a horseshoe (nailed to the mast of a
ship or a house door). The word 'knife' was not spoken at sea
but an iron knife might be stuck into a mast for good luck. Worst
of all was to see a clergyman before getting aboard, and to refer
to one other than as 'the mannie in the black coat' was to spell
doom. The fishermen of the Tweed sprinkled their nets with
salt to avert the dire consequences of a spoken taboo word like
the names of fish, and in throwing salt into the water they
believed it placated the river spirits and ensured safety of the
boats.

Arms of the Borough of Berwick-upon-Tweed

In heraldic terms the arms of the borough are described thus:
'Per pale Azure and Gules, upon a mount in base Vert, a wych-
elm Proper and in front of the same a bear passant Proper, muzzled and chained to the base of the tree with a chain Or. Below
the shield, which is ensigned of the coronet proper to a Royal

Burgh, upon a Compartment suitable to a Burgh Royal, along with this Motto *Victoria Gloria Merces*, are set for Supporters two bears Proper, muzzled and chained with chains reflexed over their backs Or' (*Lyon Register, xli,103:14 Nov 1958*).

The Royal Burgh of Berwick-upon-Tweed dates from *circa* 1124, and was one of the *Curia Quattuor Burgorum* (see page 11), the principal Burghs of the Kingdom of Scotland, finally passing from Scottish hands in 1482. In total, Berwick was captured or sacked fourteen times. The arms of the borough were granted in 1958 by Lord Lyon Sir Thomas Innes of Learney under the 'ancient user' privilege allowed under the Act of 1672. The old seals of Berwick (see page 18) indicate that Berwick did utilise a form of Arms while a Scottish Royal Burgh. Consequently, because of its history, in 1958 Berwick was granted arms of a 'Scottish flavour', which caused much controversy with the College of Arms in London. (Cf: Arms of North Berwick with their motto *Victoriae Gloria Merces*, 'Glory is the reward of victory.')

The arms of Berwick are based on traditional designs used by the town for many years. The bear and the wych-elm are a pun on the name Ber-wick, and they appear, as Marguerite Wood and J.H.Stevenson pointed out in *Scottish Heraldic Seals* (Glasgow, 1940), on municipal seals of the thirteenth and fourteenth centuries. The heraldic 'field' is parted blue (for France) and red (for England), the colours of the dual shields used from 1405 to 1603 when the arms of France were quartered with England's.

Those interested in coats of arms will find representations— on the Elizabethan walls at Marygate carpark; on Avenue House, 4 Palace Street East, where the arms of previous owners, the Call family, are displayed; and on the gateway of Ravensdowne Barracks which shows the arms of George I quartered for England and Scotland, France, Ireland and Hanover (displaying the white horse of Hanover and the gold crown of the Holy Roman Emperor Charlemagne).

Incidentally, Berwick's only remaining examples of fire marks (to show the burgh firefighters that the house was insured) are to be found at 4 Palace Green, and the former Avenue Hotel (1899: now Sidney Court).

A dukedom for Berwick

The incorporation of the name of Berwick within a dukedom was established in 1687 for James Fitz-James (1670-1734), the elder of the two illegitimate sons of King James VII & II by Arabella Churchill, sister of the famous general, the Duke of Marlborough.

James Fitz-James was educated in France, and on his father's accession he entered the Imperial army and served his military apprenticeship in Hungary under the command of the Duke of Lorraine. In 1687 he commanded the Princess Anne of Denmark's regiment, then garrisoned at Berwick. Fitz-James was congratulated on the award of his title by Berwick Town Council in a letter signed by the mayor, William Lawson.

In 1688 the new duke, who had been made a burgess of the Corporation of Berwick, accompanied his father into exile and joined the Jacobite struggle to regain the throne for the deposed James VII & II. The duke took part in the Battle of the Boyne in 1690. Later he transferred his services to France and in 1696 attempted to stir up an insurrection against William III which was a total failure. Subsequently the duke distinguished himself during the War of the Spanish Succession, defeating the allied forces under General Stanhope at Almansa. James Fitz-James was killed at the siege of Philippsburg; he left descendants both in Spain and France.

James Fitz-James's dukedom was forfeit in 1695 when he was attainted, and although it remained forfeit it was used by nine subsequent 'Dukes of Berwick', the last being Charles Maria Isabel Stuart Fitz-James (1849-1901). This duke's son discarded the title (although his father had used it when visiting Queen Victoria at Balmoral), but it occurs in more recent times in the titles of a Spanish descendant, namely Dona Maria del Rosario Cayetana Fitz-James Stuart y Silva, 18th Duchess of Alba de Tormes, Duchess of Berwick.

Berwick's histories and historians

Taking into consideration the strategic importance of Berwick down the centuries, and given also that it was one of the most valuable urban centres until late-medieval times, it is strange that historians have been, at the very least, neglectful of Berwick. The first attempt at a history of Berwick occurred only in 1799 in the record prepared by Dr John Fuller as *The History of Berwick-upon-Tweed* (Bell & Bradfute *et al*, 1799). This rambling account, which gives little real information indeed in its 601 pages plus 50 pages of appendices, was the first narrative of Berwick in volume form with a short comment on Tweedmouth and Spittal and a few observations on the land as far as Holy Island in the south and the Cheviots in the southwest. As to historical content Fuller's examination of the town is perfunctory and only really begins in the mid-twelfth century, closing with the accession of James VI & I in 1603. Fuller relied on two main sources, W.Hutchinson's *A View of Northumberland* (1778) and *The Border History of England and Scotland* (1776) written by George Ridpath, who offers still a good perspective of Berwick's medieval role. But all of these writers depended upon some doubtful earlier sources.

A graduate of St Andrews University, Fuller was practising as a surgeon at Ayton when he wrote his history, so his text is based on personal observation and local study. It appears that Fuller's text, once described as an 'old mixture of Medical Jurisprudence' and not very helpful asides, was developed from a study of Berwick which he made for Sir John Sinclair's *The Statistical Account of Scotland 1791-99*. Fuller died in 1825.

The next history of Berwick was by the Rev. Thomas Johnstone (1777-1843), minister of the Low Meeting House (1719) in Berwick's Hide Hill. He wrote *The History of Berwick-upon-Tweed* (Reid, Watson *et al*, 1817) and the vii+234 page book contained a copy of the Charter granted to the town by James VI & I. Johnstone's book should be read with caution because of its partisan and dated scholarship; he it was, for instance, who repeated Captain Francis Grose's allegation in *The Antiquities of*

Scotland(1789-91) that the Countess of Buchan 'was exhibited in a wooden cage, on the Walls of Berwick Castle...for the space of seven years....'(1306). Again in Johnstone's book several large chunks of history are left out.

Frederick Sheldon (died aged 34), the 'stage name' of William Thompson, a theatrical shopkeeper-cum-actor who was associated with Berwick theatre in the 1840s, was the next to undertake a *History of Berwick-upon-Tweed* (A.&C. Black, 1849). He observed that he was inspired to write his history both by a feeling that such a history was 'much wanted' and by an 'able account' of Berwick written by 'that indefatigable antiquary', Robert Weddell, in the *Penny Encyclopaedia* (1835). Weddell, incidentally, was a solicitor and antiquary who lived at Avenue House in Palace Street East in the 1820s, and Weddell's Lane is named after him. Sheldon's book was competent by the amateur standards of the time and as thorough as he could make it, despite his purple passages and rather theatrical comments where no records exist. He relied heavily on Fuller.

John Scott (1833-90) wrote what came nearest to being the definitive history of Berwick with his *Berwick-upon-Tweed* (Elliot Stock, 1888). Subtitled the 'History of the Town and Guild', the book is still worthy of close study, and Scott was the first to take advantage of the modern *Calendars of State Papers* which he consulted for data on foreign, domestic and Border susbjects. From 1866 John Scott was rector of the Corporation Academy in the town and remained in this post until his death. He was one of the founders of the Berwick Museum and acted as its honorary curator. He began his studies of Berwick during his preparation of material for winter lectures held in Berwick on Saturday evenings.

Undoubtedly those interested in the history of Berwick should consult the *History of the Berwickshire Naturalists' Club*. The BNC was instituted on 22 September 1831 and its *History* reflects the study of Berwick local history from 1831 to 1988. A History of the club itself is contained in the two index volumes of 1933 and 1987. The archives of the BNC are held at the Berwick Museum and may be consulted by prior arrangement.

A number of 'local guides' have been published in the last eighty years, and those worthy of particular attention are: Rev. J. King of St Mary's, *The Edwardian Walls and Elizabethan Ramparts of Berwick-on-Tweed* (1906); George L. Batty and P. Spowart's *Complete Guide to Berwick-on-Tweed* (1907); and Francis Martin Norman's *Official Guide to the Fortifications, with explanatory drawings* (1907). Commander Norman (1833-1918), of Cheviot House, was a former sheriff, mayor and alderman of the town and a president of the original borough museum. Norman presented the marble memorial fountain in Castlegate on 20 June 1897 to mark the Diamond Jubilee of Queen Victoria; the fountain displays an interesting copy of the medieval seal of Berwick's mayoralty.

By far the most prominent and knowledgeable local historian of Berwick in recent years is Francis M. Cowe of the family firm of Messrs Wm.Cowe & Sons, 64-66 Bridge Street, and his *Berwick-upon-Tweed: A short historical guide* (Revised 1984) is worthy of attention.

Berwick's Museums, Public Library and Art Gallery

Local history can be studied at the borough's museums and public library. It was a piece of happy inspiration that has grouped Berwick's main museums within the barracks at Ravensdowne. Here are to be found the Berwick-upon-Tweed Borough Museum and Art Gallery, the King's Own Scottish Borderers Regimental Museum, and the English Heritage Exhibition. English Heritage restored the eighteenth-century barracks, and their exhibition, 'By Beat of Drum', depicts the history of the British infantryman from 1660 to 1900.

Berwick's Borough Museum was a long time in gestation. A plan to open a museum at Berwick was launched in 1840, and preliminary steps to open a museum at Berwick arose from preparations for the Highland Show of 1841. The then mayor, Dr George Johnston (1797-1855), founder in 1831 and first president of the Berwickshire Naturalists' Club, appealed for funds to set up a historical exhibition. His efforts failed and the attempt to found a museum was abandoned, but eventually in 1867 it was established and was based on the by then deceased Dr Johnston's collection; the artifacts were displayed in a room at the Corn Exchange, Sandgate. By 1872 the museum was located at new premises in the High Street (Marygate), and when this site was demolished in 1882 a new museum, reading room, lecture room and art school replaced the original building. In 1920 the Victorian edifice was offered to the Town Council and an attendant was appointed at £1.50 per week when the municipal authority agreed to take it on. By 1935 an important collection was given to the borough by Sir William Burrell (1861-1958), the characterful and eccentric shipping magnate who lived at Hutton Castle. Indeed his gifts to the borough began in the very early 1930s, and in all he gave more than eight hundred items (one tenth of his entire collection) to the people of Berwick. Burrell's gifts form the nucleus of Berwick's Art Gallery displays which include items from Mesopotamia, Egypt, Greece and Rome. Berwick Art Gallery was first opened at the public library in High Street on 5 May 1949 by Sir William and Lady Burrell; Sir William himself arranged for the temperature and humidity levels to be checked. Today there are displayed pictures as catholic in taste as the works of Boudin, Degas, Monticelli and Ramsay.

During the period 1950-74 Berwick Museum and Art Gallery went through a period of astonishing public and civic neglect, but in 1974 the Local Government Reorganisation split the library and museum between the Borough and County Council, although Berwick librarians continued to look after the displays. In 1985 the Museum and Art Gallery moved to the Clock Block (1739-41) of the barracks, and at last Berwick's treasures are being displayed with professional skill by a permanent curator, with an ongoing programme of research and conservation.

On display are examples of the work of three out of four local painters. Thomas Sword Good (1739-1872) was a native of Berwick who began as a house painter; by 1815 he was exhibiting his coastal landscapes and scenes at Edinburgh. He was a member of the Berwickshire Naturalists' Club and lived at 21 Quay Walls. Good's brother Robert, not represented, was a painter and engraver. James Wallace Sr. (1841-1911) lived at 22 Quay Walls and was first art master at the Berwick Art School in 1873; James Wallace Jr. (1872-1937) was also a painter of note.

Berwick's public library is now located in nearby Church Street at the west end of The Parade.

Across the barrack square from the museum is the museum of the King's Own Scottish Borderers. The barracks was the depot of the regiment between 1881 and 1964 and the museum was refurbished in 1983. It presents the history of the regiment from its inception by Col. David Leslie, 3rd Earl of Leven, in 1689, and on display are uniforms, medals, musical instruments and ephemera associated with the regiment.

At the old Guildhall (Town Hall), Marygate, is sited the Berwick Cell Block Museum, which displays (by means of twice-daily guided tours in season) the eighteenth-century criminal cells and the reconstructed council chamber, along with a welter of local items.

The Wine and Spirit Museum is privately operated and is situated in the grounds of the Governor's House. It was established in 1978 and displays a wide range of artifacts used in wine production collected by the museum's founder, J.Michael Hackett of Lindisfarne Ltd., the makers of Lindisfarne Mead; free samples of the mead and displays of pottery (introduced in 1982) are found in the complex at the rear of the museum within the craft shop. It is open from Easter to October.

The Borough Archives

The museums and public library can supply the local historian with a great deal of social history ephemera and printed background material, particularly in the 'local history' collections. But there comes a time when the local historian needs more detailed primary sources of data on such subjects as the ancient government of the town, or the Guild of Freemen, or how Berwick fitted into the history of the two

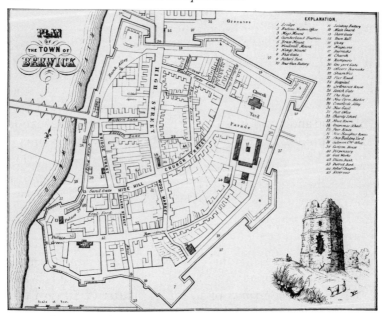

Map of Berwick from Frederick Sheldon's *History of Berwick-upon-Tweed* (1849) showing the layout of early Victorian Berwick. Shaws Lane, incidentally, is now Chapel Street, which latterly took its name from the Middle Meeting House, which had been built in 1756 as a Presbyterian church, near Crawford Alley.

nations of Scots and English, and for all this he or she must turn to the borough archives.

Berwick's archives are to be found in the Borough Council Offices, Wallace Green, in the municipal buildings built 1848-9 as a jail to supersede that at the Town Hall. Under the care of the County Archivist of Northumberland, the Berwick Record Office is open to the public each Thursday.

The borough's books and papers were first listed in a published handlist of 1872 prepared by the Rev. Joseph Stevenson, and another report on the town's manuscripts appeared in 1901 under the hand of W.D. Macray who concentrated on the early sixteenth-century Orders and Statutes relating to how the town was governed by the 'ruling class' of Freemen and the garrison officers.

Today the borough archives include the following: Charters; Guild papers; Court documents; Town Council records; Local Board of Health and Urban Sanitary Authority papers; Property records; Residents' records; Accounts; Litigation reports; Freemen and Freemen's Estate records; Education, Police, Jail and Burial Board records; documents on the Manor of Tweedmouth and Spittal; Tithes; Harbour Commissioners' reports; Railway records; Plans; Posters; Magdalene Fields Estate papers; Census 1841-81; Parish Register for Holy Trinity and Tweedmouth; Parliamentary Papers and Public Records.

By far the most important documents are the town's charters, the Guild Minutes and the Jotting Books.

Eight charters for Berwick are extant:

1. 29 November 1415. Henry V. This is the earliest of the charters and forms an *inspeximus* (copy) of the charter of Edward III, itself an *inspeximus* of an earlier charter of Edward III, again an *inspeximus* of the charter of Edward I; the latter was the governing charter of Berwick until that of James VI & I.
2. 18 February 1483. Edward IV.
3. 6 November 1486. Henry VII.
4. 19 April 1510. Henry VIII.
5. 1 June 1547. Edward VI.
6. 25 April 1554. Mary I.
7. 4 May 1559. Elizabeth I.
8. 16 April 1603. James VI & I. This charter was the governing charter of Berwick until the coming of the Reform Act of 1832. The charter was surrendered to Charles II at his request and on the promise of a new one; Charles died in 1685 and the town was promised a new charter by James VII & II, but James fled in 1688; the charter was restored by William III.

It is important to note that there are no traces in the archives of any Scottish charter, or of the mass of documents dated from Berwick or relevant to Berwick when it was the most important Royal Burgh in Scotland. It is likely that when Robert I, the Bruce, took the town in the early fourteenth century, in taking

away the charter given to the town by Edward I, he also took the
other records.

The papers referring to the Guild of Freemen (the Guild
administered the town for the Freemen, or burgesses) include
three important collections: Drafts, October 1505; Minutes, 21
June 1513; and Guild Minute Books, of which there is almost a
complete collection. The 'Jotting Books' include the Town
Clerk's Books, Letter Books, Petitions, Minutes and related
documents. All are important records of the way of life of the
Berwick folk, and it is clear that not one horse passed through
the town, and not one egg was sold, that the ubiquitous Freemen did not know about.

Berwick on maps and plans

Berwick has one of the earliest surviving town maps, and plans
and maps themselves offer the local historian a different
approach to exploring history. This is the most important
sequence of Berwick maps:
Manuscript plans of Elizabethan Berwick. 1570.
These were prepared by Rowland Johnson, the Surveyor of
Works at Berwick, 1565-*circa* 1575.
Six plans are held at Hatfield House, Hertfordshire.
1. Plan endorsed by Sir Richard Lees Cardes of Barwicke and
signed R.Johnson.
2. Plan similarly endorsed.
3. Plan signed by R.Johnson (see: Tenison, E.M. *Elizabethan
England*).
4. Manuscript endorsed 'The Boundes of Barwyk'. R.Johnson.
5. Platte of the town & Castle of Barwicke—amended by
Antonio da Bergomo.
6. Plan attributed to Rowland Johnson.
(see: Skelton, R.A. & Summerson, J. *A Description of Maps*
(Roxburghe Club, 1971)).
The True Description of Her Majesty's town of Berwick. Circa 1590.
This plan, by an anonymous cartographer, appears in John
Scott's *Berwick-upon-Tweed* (1888), at page 172, and shows the

extent of the medieval wall, the Elizabethan walls, the line of the Catwell wall, the castle, the pre-1611-34 bridge (with fortified gateway towards the Tweedmouth side), the pier, the open area of the Greenses and the plain church of Holy Trinity. A copy is held at the National Library of Scotland.

Map of the lands granted by the Charter of James VI & I. 1603.
Survey of November 1603, including the Liberties of Berwick. Appears in Scott's *Berwick* (at page 327). National Library of Scotland holds copy.

Inset on John Speed's map of Northumberland. 1610.
Within 'The Theatre of the Empire of Great Britaine (1611)'. Based on the map of 1590.
(See: Fordham, A. *Town Plans of the British Isles*).

Berwick. 1706.
By V.M.Coronelli. In Vol.3. 'Teatro della Guerra' and in 'Atatante Veneto'.

Anonymous plan of Berwick's (demolished) fortifications. 1725.

Anonymous plan of fortifications of 1310-20 and walls of circa 1560.
Appears in Scott's *Berwick* at page 142. Shows how the castle was linked to the defences and the town.

Barwic. 1757.
By J.N.Bellin. In 'Essai Géographique sur les Isles Britanniques'.

A plan inset on County Map of Northumberland. 1769.
By Captain Andrew Armstrong (d.1791) and his son Mostyn John Armstrong.

Boundary Map. Circa 1806.
In Cambridge University Library.

Berwick. 1821.
Inset in John Thomson's map of Berwickshire.

Map. 1822.
By John Wood in his 'Town Atlas of Scotland'. Wood, who died in 1847, was a land surveyor of Canaan Grove, Greenhill, Edinburgh; he had surveyed Berwick personally in 1822.

The Ordnance Survey offer this set of maps of Berwick significance:

6″ to 1 mile County Series: Berwick Sheet 18. 1st Edition, 1862.

25″ to 1 mile County Series: Berwickshire 18/12. 1st Edition, 1861.

6″ to 1 mile County Series, ¼ sheets. Northumberland/4NW/4SW. 1898 Edition.

25″ to 1 mile County Series. Northumberland 4/5 and 4/9. 1898 Edition.

6″ to 1 mile County Series (New Series), ¼ sheets. Northumberland 2SW. Editions of 1926 & 1939.

25″ to 1 mile County Series (New Series). Northumberland 2/14. 1924 Edition.

And current series.

These may be obtained from: The Ordnance Survey, Romsey Road, Maybush, Southampton SO9 4DH.

In looking for maps and plans of Berwick, it is worthwhile to search for such plans as were prepared for civil engineers like Thomas Telford (1757-1834). For instance, two items are of particular interest:

Book of reference to the map of the mail road from Edinburgh to Morpeth through Berwick. 1824; plans 1825.

Report...relative to the proposed railway from Glasgow to Berwick-upon-Tweed. 1810.

Useful maps of Berwick's walls appear in Iain Macivor's *The Fortifications of Berwick-upon-Tweed* (**HMSO**, 1983).

See also: R.Neville Hadock, 'A Map of Medieval Northumberland & Durham', *Archaeologia Aeliana*. 4th Series. Vol 16, 1939, pp. 148-218; and, *A Descriptive List....Maps of Northumberland 1576-1900* by H.Whitaker.

History in newspapers and magazines

Berwick's local papers are an invaluable source of information for the local historian bent on piecing together the life and times of the town. The early newspapers, while giving a great deal of 'world' news, were interlarded with very useful notes on local events. An eye, too, to the births, marriages and deaths notices, the advertisements (for data on contemporary goods, prices and traders), the letters columns (for opinion and emotional reaction to events), the visual record of people and places when photographs began, and the snippets on sport, social life, local politics and industry all provide useful information in building up a contemporary picture of the town.

These newspaper sources are the most helpful:

The Berwick Gazette and Berwick Advertiser was first issued on 2 January 1808 (price 6d) from the publishing offices of Henry Richardson in Church Street. A few years later the newspaper was moved to Western Lane where it remained until 1900; in 1900 the Black Bull Tavern was rebuilt at 90 Marygate and its former site is now the head office of the Tweeddale Press Group who run the paper in its modern form. Since 1868 the newpaper has been under the proprietorship of the Smail family, who also commenced *The Berwickshire Advertiser* in 1893. Perhaps the *Berwick Advertiser's* most celebrated editor was the Liberal radical John Mackay Wilson (see page 156), who used his position on the paper to promote Earl Grey and the cause of Reform. *The Berwickshire Advertiser* and the *Berwick Advertiser* merged and from 1 March 1983 the *Berwick Advertiser* and the *Berwickshire News and East Lothian Advertiser* merged to link both sides of the Border.

The Berwick and Kelso Warder first appeard in 1836 to continue until January 1859 when it became *The Berwick Warder*. In September 1884 the name was changed to *The Border Counties Gazette*. Discontinued in 1899, it was merged with *The Berwick Mercury*, a free weekly issued by George Martin.

The Illustrated Berwick Journal was first issued on 16 June 1855 by William Davidson and George Turner of 43 Western Lane, priced 2d. Prior to its publication a forerunner, the *Berwick Monthly Journal*, ran to six issues. The former became the *Berwick Journal* and was ultimately owned by the Steven family who also ran *The Berwickshire News* (1869).

The Berwick Bulletin began in March 1978 and merged in the same year with the *Jedburgh Herald* to become the *Border Bulletin*. Collections of these papers are available for study at: The Central Library, Edinburgh City Libraries (*Berwick Advertiser, Berwick Bulletin, Berwick and Kelso Warder, Berwick Journal,* and

Berwickshire Advertiser) and the National Library of Scotland (*Berwick Advertiser,* *Berwick and Kelso Warder*, *Berwickshire Advertiser*); and the Berwick Public Library holds copies of the *Berwick Journal* and *Berwick Advertiser* from the issues of the 1860s.

Some snatches of local history and local contemporary thought can be gleaned from *The Berwick Museum* (or 'Monthly Literary Intelligencer'), published by William Phorson of West Street from January 1785; the magazine ran until 1787. *The Border Magazine* too was issued monthly from November 1831 until December 1832 and was published by John Rennison of 46 Marygate. The magazine also appeared in 1880-81 and again from 1896, and contained comment on contemporary events and published a 'popular three part history' of the town.

The *Berwick Leader* (1984), bylined 'The free Newspaper for Berwick and the Eastern Borders', is useful for additional current assessment of Berwick's life and times as they happen.

Further Reading

ANDERSON, A.O., 1908. *Scottish Annals from English Chroniclers AD 500-1286.*

ANON., 1840. Surtees Society. Jordan Fantosme's *Chronicle of the War between the English and the Scots in 1173 & 1174.*

BAIN, J., 1881. *Calendar of Documents Relating to Scotland.* Vols I-IV, 1108-1509.

BARROW, G.W.S., 1981. *Kingship and Unity: Scotland 1000-1306.*

COLVIN, H.M. (ed.), 1963. *History of the Kings Works.* Vols 1-2.

COWAN, I.B. and EASSON, D.E., 1976. *Mediaeval Religious Houses* (Scotland). 2nd ed.

Denham Tracts. 1858.

DONNELLY, J., 1980. 'Thomas of Coldingham, merchant and burgess of Berwick (d.1316)'. *Scottish Historical Review.*

DOUGLAS, R. 1875. *Sketch of the History of Berwick Grammar School.*

DUNCAN, A.A.M., 1978. *Scotland, the Making of the Kingdom.*

ELLISON, M., 1976. 'An Archaeological Survey of Berwick-upon-Tweed', in *Archaeology in the North* (Clack, P.A.G & Gosling, P.F., eds.).

FINDEN, E.W., 1838. *Views of Ports and Harbours.*

FULLER, J., 1799. *The History of Berwick-upon-Tweed.*

GREY, Sir Thomas, 1836. *Scalachronica.*

HIGHAM, N., 1986. *The Northern Counties to AD 1000.*

HOLT, T.G., 1983. 'Berwick-upon-Tweed: the Story of a Legacy'. *Northern Catholic History*, No.18.

HUNTER, J.R., 'Medieval Berwick-upon-Tweed'. *Archaeologia Aeliana.* Series 5, Vol. 15, 1982.

LAMONT-BROWN, R., 1972. *General Trade in Berwick-upon-Tweed 1894.*

LAMONT-BROWN, R., 1971. 'Witches and Witchcraft: Superstition in the Eastern Borders'. *History of the Berwickshire Naturalists' Club.* Vol XXXIX.

MACKENZIE, W.M. 1945. *Scottish Burghs.*

MACIVOR, I., 1965. 'The Elizabethan Fortifications of Berwick-upon-Tweed'. *Antiquaries Journal.*

MAXWELL, H., 1913. *The Chronicle of Lanercost.*

MOIR, D.G., 1983. *The Early Maps of Scotland.*

PEVSNER, N., 1957. *Northumberland.*

PRYDE, G.S., 1965. *The Burghs of Scotland.*

RAINE, J.R., 1852. *History....North Durham.*

RIDLEY, J., 1968. *John Knox.*

RIDPATH, G., 1776. *Border History.*

RITCHIE, R.L.G., 1954. *The Normans in Scotland.*

SCOTT, J., 1888. *Berwick-upon-Tweed.*

SCOTT, Sir W., 1822. *Halidon Hill.*

SHELDON, F., 1849. *History of Berwick.*

SKENE, W.F. 9ed.), 1872. John of Fordun's *Chronicle of the Scottish Nation.*

STEWART, I.H., 1955. *The Scottish Coinage.*

STUART, J. and BURNETT, G., 1978. *The Exchequer Rolls of Scotland.*

SYKES, J., 1866. *Local Records.*

TIBBETTS, K., 1962. 'Methodism in Berwick-on-Tweed'. *Wesley Historical Society Proceedings*, XXXIII.

WALLACE, H.M., 1931. 'Berwick in the Reign of Elizabeth'. *English Historical Review*, 46.

WATT, D.E.R. (ed.),1987. Walter Bower's *Scotichronicon.*

WHITE, K.G., 1962-63. 'The Spades Mire, Berwick-upon-Tweed'. *Proceedings of the Society of Antiquaries of Scotland*, 96.

Index

Abbey St. Bathans,31
Abernethy,9
*Accounts of the Collectors of the Thirds of
Benefices,*168
Aethelfrith, king,5
Agricola, Gnaeus Julius,2
Ailred of Rievaulx,9
Alauna (Learchild),3
Alexander I,10
Alexander II,17,20,25,26,28,33
Alexander III,20,25,28,29,40,162
Alfred, king,7
Allanbank,3
Alnwick,3,4,14,113
Amersham, Sir Walter of,46
Anglians,4-5
Anglo Saxons,7
Anne, queen,109,113
Ardern, Richard,84
Aston, John,100
Attacotti,4

Baird, Rev.J,196
Baker, Geoffrey de,62
Baldersbury,71
Balliol, John, king,26,34,41,42-
44,46,47
Bamburgh,4,5,8,9,60
Bannockburn, battle of,45,51,62
Barbour, John,21,51
Bartholomew, Roger of Berwick,42
*Battle of Otterbourne,*67
Bede, the Venerable,6
Bernham, David de (Bishop of St
Andrews),33,39
Bernicia,4-5,7
Berwick, Treaty of,66-67,81,90
Berwick Artillery Volunteers,89
Berwick Cockles,140,152
Berwick Corporation (Freemen) Trus-
tees,119,144-47
Berwick Naturalists'
Club,18,63,102,130,202
Berwick Preservation Trust,148-151
Berwick Rangers,102
BERWICK-UPON-TWEED:
Amateur Rowing Club,37
archives,205-207

arms,196-197
art gallery,204-205
banks,174-177
barracks,109,111,116,119,123,131,
203,205
batardeau,84,88
boundaries,68-72
burgh warden,15
byepass,161
Calf Hill,93
castle,14-16,17,20-25,35,41,42,44,45,
46,50,52,53,66,103,136
Castle Vale Park,17,22,23,55
cattle market,87
chamberlain,19,21,27,49
charities,129
charters,207,208
churches: Anti-Burgher Meeting
House,125
Augustinian,35-36
Bankhill United Reformed
Church,126
Baptist Meeting House,126
Burgher Meeting House,125
Carmelite,35,50,52
Dominican (Blackfriars),34-35,75
Franciscan (Greyfriars),33-34,75
Friars of the Penitence,35
Halyston Cistercian nunnery,30-
31,43,64,65
High Meeting House,124
Holy Trinity,18,24,38-39,71,77,92;
of 1648-50, 93,97,101,102,123
Holy Trinity on Berwick
Bridge,35,39
Low Meeting House,124,201
Methodist Meeting House,126,127
Our Lady & St Cuthbert (RC)
church,128,160
Ravensdale,35,36
Relief (Middle) Meeting House,126
St Aidan's,126
St Andrew's,124
St Lawrence,38
St Mary's (Castlegate),138
St Mary's (Scotsgate),37,39,71,87
St Nicholas,38,39
Segden Hermitage,35,70

215